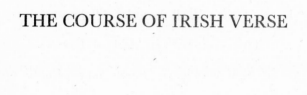

THE COURSE OF IRISH VERSE

THE COURSE OF IRISH VERSE
IN ENGLISH

By

ROBERT FARREN

NEW YORK

SHEED AND WARD

1947

Printed in the United States of America

To

SEUMAS BRENNAN

Most selfless of men

ACKNOWLEDGMENTS

I gratefully acknowledge the kindness of all those named hereunder in granting me permission to use copyright poems or extracts from poems or prose as illustrations to my text:

The Macmillan Company and Mr. Diarmuid Russell, for quotations from "Immortality," "Remembrance," "Carrowmore," "A Call of the Sidhe" and "Reconciliation," all from *Collected Poems,* by A.E. (George Russell).

The Macmillan Company and Mrs. W. B. Yeats, for quotations from *Essays,* by W. B. Yeats.

The Macmillan Company and Mr. Pádraic Colum, for quotations from "The Ballad of Roger Casement," "The Terrible Robber Man," "Girls Spinning" and "The Poor Girl's Meditation," all from *Collected Poems,* by Pádraic Colum.

The Macmillan Company and Mr. James Stephens, for quotations from "The Dancer," "The Chill of the Eve," "The Shell," "To the Four Courts, Please," "Behind a Hill" and "Clann Cartie," all from *Collected Poems,* by James Stephens.

The Macmillan Company and Mr. Austin Clarke, for quotations from "The Lost Heifer," "Aisling" and "The Young Woman of Beare," all from *Collected Poems,* by Austin Clarke; also Mr. Clarke for quotations from "The Blackbird of Derrycairn" and "No story handed down in Connacht," from *As the Crow Flies* and *Night and Morning,* respectively.

Random House, Inc., for quotations from the following poems by John Millington Synge: "Queens," "Danny," "The Passing of the Shee."

Mrs. F. R. Higgins and Macmillan and Company, London, England, for quotations from the following poems by the late F. R. Higgins: "To My Blackthorn Stick," "The Three-cornered

Field," "A Vision of Paradise Park," "The Ghost," "A Sheiling of the Music."

Dr. James Starkey ("Seumas O'Sullivan"), for quotations from: "The Twilight People," "The Poplars," "O Herdsman, driving your slow, twilight flock" and "The Others," all from *Dublin Poems,* published by The Creative Age Press.

Mr. Simon Campbell, for quotations from: "The Nine-penny Fidil," "I will go with my father a-ploughing," "The Gilly of Christ" and " 'Tis pretty tae be in Baile-liosain," all from *The Mountainy Singer,* by Joseph Campbell.

Lord Dunsany, for permission given on behalf of the family of the late Francis Ledwidge, to quote from: "The Blackbirds" and "The Dream of Aengus," both in *Collected Poems,* by Francis Ledwidge, published by Herbert Jenkins, Ltd., London, England.

The Talbot Press, Dublin, Ireland, for quotations from "A Song for Mary Magdalen," by P. H. Pearse.

CONTENTS

PREFACE

This book began as an appendix to a larger book, a study of the translators into English of Irish Gaelic poetry. In the appendix I intended to outline the history of original Irish poetry in English, insofar as it is complementary to the study of the translators. But I found it impossible to keep my appendix within reasonable limits of size, and eventually decided to make of it a separate book, and to publish it before revising the larger study.

Only two other things need be said. The first is this: the present book, to the best of my belief and endeavour, is complete in itself, and may be read without reference to the forthcoming study of the translation movement; though of course when both are available they will be complementary in a general way. The second thing to be said is this: I am not in this relatively short outline attempting a history of Anglo-Irish verse; or even complete evaluations of the poets with whom I deal. My purpose is more restricted: it is to show, as my title declares, the course of Irish poetry in the English language; to observe and remark upon the growth in Irishness, in separate existence from English poetry, of the poetry that was and is composed in Ireland or by Irishmen. I have, I believe, treated of all the important poets, and some of the less important, who have claims to be considered; but not as subjects in themselves. Yeats, for instance, could not possibly be estimated or described in the space I have given him;

but perhaps that space is reasonable in relation to my theme.

I have, I confess, dilated upon several poets somewhat beyond the strictest needs of my subject, and with them essayed something resembling integral evaluation and description. Mangan, F. R. Higgins and Austin Clarke are the chief of these; and my reason for giving extra space to them is this: that their measure of poetic achievement and importance to Irish poetry seem to me out of all proportion to the attention they have hitherto received.

That is the end of my prefacing, except that I must thank Mr. Brinsley MacNamara for assistance derived from his exact and knowledgeable reading of my proofs.

POETRY IN ENGLISH WAS ATTEMPTED IN IRELAND AS early as the fourteenth century; but genius did not, we might say, engage in this attempt till Edmund Spenser composed his *Faerie Queen* at Kilcolman Castle. Irishmen hardly brought genius to the work till the start of the eighteenth century; for, most Irish poets until then—and for more than half a century after—wrote in Irish. The first great writers of English in our race were Swift, Goldsmith, Berkeley, Burke and Sheridan.

Goldsmith and Sheridan, though Irish by birth and race, were virtually English writers. Sheridan possibly paraphrased one Gaelic song; he certainly wrote one play with an Irish title and created some "Irish" characters; besides which he employed eloquence and wit which some (A. E. among them) thought to be distinctively and persistently Irish; yet the Irishness of Sheridan is more gainsaid than conceded. Doubtless no writer entirely erases the marks of his youth's environment; hence there are those who, possibly with truth, remark in Goldsmith Irish qualities; it remains, however, no simple task to isolate in the body of his work distinctively Irish moments.

Swift is in different case. His special temperament— his choler and his itch to rule; his lengthy, though enforced (more potent, possibly, because it was enforced) residence in Ireland; his girding at his wrongs and the wrongs of others; the heady thanks and worship of the

Dublin mob—all these circumstances joined to make of him, politically and socially, an Irish writer, in content at least; and the newness of the content drives this home. Moreover his wittily ferocious lampoons are, in their whole-hog fury, markedly un-English, and they become increasingly un-English as they darken from Bickerstaff-baiting to the rending and mauling of Man the Cosmic Yahoo.

But of course, of course, he has many traits not Irish; again—with many more *of course's*—he wished to write like, and principally for, certain Englishmen, Pope, Arbuthnot and Gay; while finally—with a very stormflood of *of course's*—he would not have comprehended (or would have writhed and mocked) had any contemporary said he wrote, or ought to write, with an Irish pen. At one point certainly, perhaps at a second, he touched Gaelic letters. That is, he made an English version of *O Rourke's Feast,* a poem by Hugh MacGowran; and some say that *Gulliver's Travels* was suggested by the Gaelic tale of *Eisirt.*

Berkeley and Burke were, by every literary measurement, all but English writers, though the bishop from the first regarded himself as Irish.

Here then are the first points about our literature in English:

That it started with a handful of geniuses;

That two of them, Burke and Goldsmith, can scarcely have escaped some knowledge of the Irish language;

That Swift only of the group may be said to have decidedly Irish features—chiefly political and social thought about Ireland, and a fierceness in satire which the English have rarely and we very often.

We are hardly concerned with the orators of the Irish Bar and Parliament, except to note that theirs was another distinguished use of English which dealt with Irish affairs. We are on the other hand very much concerned, though only for an instant, with those who linked the older and the newer writing together. I mean the men who translated Gaelic verse into English.

The earliest translators had little that was Gaelic in their work. They were led to translate our verse because Keating and other prose-writers were already translated; because, as well, they used to hear the Gaelic-speaking countryfolk saying and singing the older poetry around them. But their theory of translation, the impress of Macpherson, and their immersion in English modes of writing, all prevented more than the single step—of translating, rather than inventing "Celtic" poetry. Yet that was a long step, indeed, and it took us into fruitful country.

There was, quite surely, in the poetry in English which Irish poets were writing around them, nothing to suggest an Irish mode for translation. Charlotte Brooke's *Reliques* appeared in 1789, when she was forty-nine; and she died in 1793, when Thomas Moore was ten; she might just possibly have read John Philpot Curran's

3

If sadly thinking, with spirits sinking,
Could, more than drinking, my cares compose,

the internal rhyming and unbroken roll of which were
Gaelic facets (for Curran spoke Irish as a native); but
apart from that song there were only such poets as Edward
MacLysaght (alleged to have written one of his songs in
both Irish and English) and Cork's Dick Millikin. Millikin was twenty-three when the *Reliques* appeared, hence
a youth when they were being written; so even his *Groves
of Blarney,* composed in mockery of hedge-schoolmasters'
English verse, but catching the Gaelic motion and "vowelling" which *they* were preserving, even *that* Miss Brooke
would not have known.

This hedge-schoolmaster verse, since I mention it,
should be noted as among the earliest verse to echo Irishly;
but, being largely anonymous, and written by a well-
scorned class, it provided no model for the Charlotte
Brookes of Ireland.

II

CHARLOTTE BROOKE WAS DEAD IN 1793. IN 1808, WHEN
he was twenty-nine, Moore began publishing his *Irish
Melodies,* and in two or three of these, for the first time,
an important poet was influenced by Gaelic song—not
indeed by the language or its verse, for he knew neither,
but by the music to which it was sung; and the effect was

the same. Students are quite familiar with two of the poems—*At the Mid Hour of Night* and *The Irish Peasant to his Mistress*—in which such critics as Thomas Mac-Donagh have remarked rhythms which until then no important poet ever made in English:

> At the mid hour of night when stars are weeping I fly
> To the lone vale we loved when youth shone warm in thine
>   eye;
> And I think oft, if spirits can steal from the regions of air
> To revisit past scenes of delight, thou wilt come to me there,
> And tell me our love is remembered, even in the sky.
>
> Then I sing the wild song 'twas once such pleasure to hear,
> When our voices, commingling, breathed, like one, on the
>   ear;
> And, as Echo far off through the vale my sad orison rolls,
> I think, O my love! 'tis thy voice, from the Kingdom of
>   Souls,
> Faintly answering still the notes that once were so dear.

One can match that rhythm, and that stanza, many times in Irish, but not in the English of any poet of England. The length of the lines, their unemphatic stresses (which recall the characteristic "touch" of French verse), and the highly-characteristic fifth line in the stanza, might puzzle all but the very open-eared and auditorily-imaginative English reader, but not the reader who has read Gaelic *amhrán* appreciatively. The fifth line is that exquisite departure from obtrusive, and therefore cloying, symmetry, which parallels the musician's occasional dissonance in the midst of harmony; or, to go deeper for its warrant, which parallels the slight, delightful asymmetries of natural shapes, human, animal and still. It was the need of some such asymmetry which Chesterton felt, when he said that after gazing long on the Elgin marbles one longed for a touch of ugliness, or the need which the ordinary man and woman feel when they say a face is "too perfect" in feature. They want some dissonance to enrich the harmony.

Apart from these two songs, acute inspection of Moore's *Melodies* will reveal others with a Gaelic flavour. Such, I believe, is *Silent, O Moyle,* at least in some of its lines. Such is *While gazing on the moon's light,* which, robbed of its tune, would make a worrying piece of scansion for anyone unaccustomed to the Gaelic trick of concluding lines with two or three monosyllabic feet:

> While gazing on the *moon's light*
> A moment from her smile I turned,
> To look at orbs that, *more bright,*
> In lone and distant glory burned.
> But *too far*
> Each *proud star,*
> For me to feel its warming flame;
> Much *more dear*
> That *mild sphere*
> Which near our planet smiling came . . .

Every italicized word should be strongly stressed. I admit there is nothing in the lines which, apart from the music, compels this stressing; but agreeable or reasonable scansion there is none, without it.

It is difficult, too, not to see in *To Ladies' Eyes* a rapider whirling and glinting of the dagger of rhythm than one is used to in English poetry; and the melody insists upon an emphasis in the first and third feet of every second line, which does not belong to English metres.

> To Ladies' eyes around, boy,
>> We *can't* refuse, we *can't* refuse,
> Though bright eyes so abound, boy,
>> 'Tis *hard* to choose, 'tis *hard* to choose.
> For thick as stars that lighten
>> Yon *airy* bowers, yon *airy* bowers
> The countless eyes that brighten
>> This *earth* of ours, this *earth* of ours.

Finally, why has no one (so far as I know) discovered in the following lines the voice of Gaeldom breaking in?

> Oh ye dead! Oh ye dead! whom we know by the light you give
> From your cold gleaming eyes, though you move like men who live,
>> Why leave you thus your graves,
>> In far-off fields and waves,
> Where the worm and the sea-bird only know your bed,
>> To haunt the spot where all
>> Those eyes that wept your fall,
> And the hearts that bewailed you, like your own, lie dead?

7

Cast this suddenly into the midst of an Irish connoisseurs' conversation, asking who wrote it. I should expect all but the better-memoried to agree on Mangan.

These are the specially arresting lyrics, the ones in which the Irish modality is very marked; in the *Melodies* as a whole one finds (and ascribes to the music's influence) intensity above Moore's common level. The tunes for which he wrote new lyrics have the same consuming fervour as the Gaelic lyrics, made-for or made-before those tunes. Moreover they have a compass of mood which, drawing to many of its points the sensitive Moore, drew Anglo-Irish poetry through him, and so added many courses to the few it had sailed. Looking through Crofton Croker's *Popular Songs,* or any similar anthology, we see that Anglo-Irish verse, until Moore's advent, was either mawkish or else stage-Irishly and clownishly frisky. Andrew Cherry's song *There's a dear little plant,* first sung in public in 1806, two years before the first of the *Melodies,* may represent the mawkish kind; the innumerable songs about whiskey, and *The Sprig of Shillelagh,* the second. Again we must note that some of the anonymous street-ballads, such as *Shule Aroon,* ran counter to these, as did also that tiny, but notable batch of Dublin-Villonesque verses, of which *The Night before Larry was stretched* is the best-known sample, and of which Sir John Gilbert, in his three-volume *History of Dublin,* has recorded other specimens. But the dear little shamrocks and the whiskey whoopee were the mainspring of Irish verse

8

in English till Moore wrote passionate, melancholy, dignified and gleeful songs as for an adult nation. Before him even the patriotic William Drennan has one bare hint, no more, of Gaelic influence: the heptasyllabic *Wake of William Orr*.

The Dublin of the day was feeling the debility of the Union of 1800; so Moore's achievements are more striking than his sins of omission; still it is a pity this accomplished metrist did not take fuller note of what had happened to his verse. He never lacked originality, but, had he not turned aside from his own innovations, he might have developed a more distinctive voice. His effect upon Irish poets would then have been far more native and fecundating; he might perhaps have taught the Hardiman team —especially his disciple, Thomas Furlong, to translate much nearer to the Gaelic. But "the man was thin" says Stopford Brooke (in one of the most just and percipient evaluations of Moore that I know); so his impress came from the general body of his graceful, dainty but un-Irish poetry.

III

FOR A WHILE THERE WAS NO OTHER TO EDGE translators towards closer imitation, no poet who by borrowing should give Gaelic ways repute. The poets of the time were Dermody, Lover, Lever, Darley, Sir Aubrey de Vere, Charles Wolfe and so forth; and none of them helped. Dermody was poor, both ways. Lover and Lever wrote Handy-Andy songs. Darley had a strong poetic vein and one of Irish loyalty, but they did not mingle. His "references to Irish history and his use of clan-names are colourless and weak." He was really a loss, like Moore.

For Darley could modify metres, and one of his songs gave Meredith his rhythm for *Love in the Valley*. He fooled Palgrave with a "Cavalier" lyric which would fool us all by its style if we did not know the authorship. He went nearer than most of his century's poets towards writing stageworthy plays in verse; in particular, he chose before any one the fine subject of Thomas à Becket, thereby (I believe) leading Aubrey de Vere, Tennyson and ultimately Eliot to set hands to it. Yet he drew no draught from Irish poetry, nor poured in any. He might have helped, but did not. Some may see the Irishman in his rhythmic volatility, in his thickly-pigmented images, or in his gift for rhyming on sorcery; but these arguments would equally buy us polytechnic Coleridge. Darley did not help.

Charles Wolfe, and Sir Aubrey de Vere, grandfather of the better-known Aubrey, were others without Irish tincture. Carleton's strong ballad *Sir Turlough, or The Churchyard Bridal* is possibly Irish in subject and mood, though it differs little from several ballads in Percy's *Reliques*. Besides Carleton was still a while away: his effective writing begins round 1827.

There were anticipatory flickers: there always are. I

have mentioned Philpot Curran's song; and very like it, in roll and internal rhyme, is "Father Prout's" *Bells of Shandon*. Still, "Prout" is distinctly the non-contributor; a polyglot and *belle-lettrist* of patent ability, his ear hummed always with the *Songs of Italy*, the *Songs of France*, the *Songs of Béranger*—the songs of anywhere and anyone save those of Ireland and Irishmen, except when he chipped Tom Moore or made Millikin flummery. Provoking indeed is the thought of what this ringer of changes upon European bells might have done, had he stuck to the bells of Ireland. There will always be ringers for Europe's bells, and "Prout's" dilletante nit-wittery in Paris and London could have been spared. It was an age of thwarted and squandered talent, and William Maginn, just such another as Prout, who might have meant much at home, sparked and sputtered wittily and wastefully abroad.

Another flash is in Joseph Francis Waller. He wrote the still-sung *Spinning-wheel* which, running like treadle and wheel, goes Irishly, with lines of eleven syllables:

> Mellow the moonlight to shine is beginning,
> Close by the window young Eileen is spinning;
> Bent o'er the fire her blind grandmother, sitting,
> Is crooning and groaning and drowsily knitting.

Not great verse, but a melodious, racy song, like another of Waller's, *Kitty Neil*, in which internal rhyme, carried four times through a line and a half in each octave-stanza, gives the Gaelic tone:

Ah sweet Kitty Neil, rise up from that wheel,
Your neat little foot will be weary from spinning.
Come trip down with me to the sycamore tree;
Half the parish is there, and the dance is beginning.
The sun is gone down, but the full harvest moon
Shines sweetly and cool in the dew-whitened valley;
While all the air rings with the soft loving things
Each little bird sings in the green-shaded valley.

IV

I REMIND MYSELF THAT IT WAS PROGRESS TO HAVE IRISH *matter* so common in our verse by the start of the nineteenth century. There was a time when even themes were un-Irish in our English-writing poets.

The common Irishman came early into it; but, partly because "natives" are always comic to the colonial, partly because the French Revolution had not yet made the common man matter for serious literature,* for these two reasons the common Irishman in verse inhabited Donnybrook Fair exclusively. Tadhg and Pat and Sheila were rakes, drolls, "wits", Handy Andys and Biddy Moriartys—or at best Irish emigrants and Colleen Bawns. Irish history had come in through prose translations of Keating and others; and Macpherson, Byron, Scott, Wordsworth

---

* Roughly speaking literature, being written by other classes, up to the nineteenth century, was written *about* other classes.

and others persuaded Anglo-Irish poets of the propriety of singing the beauty of Ireland which, outside verse, they had never ignored. Among them was Sir Aubrey de Vere; sonnets by him on Glengariff, The Sea-cliffs of Kilkee, Kilmallock and Castleconnel will be found in *The Dublin Book of Irish Verse.* Deservedly; de Vere was a poet and knew somewhat of sonnets. But his properties, including his mythology, are the same as his English contemporaries'. Still, it was progress when such men wrote of Ireland.

It was very tangible progress when such as Thomas Furlong found that Irishmen had for centuries written of Ireland, and done it in relishable poetry. It was not however to be thought-of that fine fellows like Furlong should go to school to the Gael, whose descendants were so ragged and unkempt. Even Gerald Griffin (1803-1840), who was born in Limerick and must surely have known Irish, did not go to the older school. Instead, at twenty, he was off to London in the wake of Sheridan, Goldsmith, Burke, Darley and Moore. Still, there are specks of Irishness in his verse, as when he makes an English song (not a translation) of *Eileen Aroon,* and uses a Gaelic phrase as refrain. His novel *The Collegians* deals of course with Irish people, including peasants.

Griffin was a Catholic, and that reminds us to trace another inflow to the subject-matter of Anglo-Irish poetry.

Swift, Steele, Parnell, Berkeley, Goldsmith, Sheridan, Burke, Grattan—almost all the grandees of our writing for its first long century, and the master part of them for

13

most of its second—Darley, Lover, Lever, Allingham, Ferguson, Le Fanu, Davis, Mitchel, Edgeworth—were Protestants; even in the first thirty years of our own century they were still the leaders: Hyde, Yeats, Shaw, Lady Gregory, Synge, O'Casey. The first halt to the treading-down of the Catholic was called in 1829, with Emancipation; but the uprising was hard, and the Famine slowed and half-crippled it. Not even yet is our writing as Catholic as our population, though the equilibrium is in sight. At the outset, then, of the nineteenth century one looks for no more than specks of Catholic writing—in English, of course: Gaelic literature is Catholic in grain.

Moore was a Catholic, but hardly one in his verse, except for the allegorical *Irish Peasant to his Mistress;* and his defection was felt. Callanan, The Banims, Griffin, Mangan, Prout, Edward Walsh, Denis Florence MacCarthy, and Aubrey de Vere after his conversion, were Catholics. But of these only Mangan, Callanan, Walsh and de Vere had real mettle; Mangan alone challenges Moore, and Mangan's best work is not overtly religious. Thus Catholic verse in nineteenth-century Ireland is sparse and thin. (So, for that matter, and with less justification, is distinctively Protestant verse.) Let us see it in process.

Banim, in his weak, sentimental song of the priest, *Soggarth Aroon,* was among the first to make a ripple. In Callanan's book there are some well-meant but tepid poems on Our Lady and The Blessed Sacrament. Walsh translated nothing but Jacobite lyrics and love-songs, unless *An raibh tu ag an gCarraig,* be, as to some it is, an allegory on the Sacred Host. Griffin, of course, was devout, and wrote some devotional verse; but he abandoned poetry on entering the Christian Brothers, and died two years after entering. Nothing of his in verse has force, but there is one subject he was the first to rhyme, a subject still without definitive treatment in poetry. Griffin's poem is *Orange and Green,* and its theme the clash of Catholic and Orangeman in Ulster. In the Six Counties this is still a living, grievous, grotesque and comic reality, yet its master poem is still unmade. Impeccable exhortations to both sides abound, in peccant verse; but only satire has been racy about them. *The Ould Orange Flute* is among the few political and poetical instants of sanity they found. Great verse and funny verse—no third kind—can safely ventilate an emotion so scalding and unyielding; and, failing great verse, funny verse has won.

In Mangan, rather curiously, one gets little of the Faith outside what comes into the poems he translates—

> The priests are on the ocean green
> They march along the deep,
> There's wine from the royal Pope
> Upon the ocean green . . .

There are, however, rare darts of devotion, like that in *The Nameless One:*

> He fled for shelter to God, who mated
> His soul with song.

Nothing of account, however; the one poem with a genuinely Christian subject which he made is a version of *St. Patrick's Breastplate.*

From the quizzical, footling, book-stuffed "Prout" we get just one touch, fleeting, but signifying the emancipation which training in Rome had bestowed on an Irish Catholic, at a time when most of his kind were self-conscious or craven. I speak of his allusions to Rome and Notre Dame in *Bells of Shandon,* which, in their very casualness, are moments of untroubled Catholic life. A Catholic layman, in being more fervent than "Prout," would, paradoxically, have been less free; in this casual Catholicism there is a calm acceptance of the place and the power of the Church, which could not have come from Callanan or Mangan.

"Prout's" acceptance resulted from acquaintance with the Church in her high places. A different kind of untroubled acceptance can spring from immersion in our countryside. For this, a poet who was very small beer, John Keegan (1809-1849), had the twin advantages of peasant origin and hedge-school teaching; hence the easy, natural glances at the Faith in *The Irish Reaper's Harvest Hymn,* addressed to Our Lady, and in *Caoch O Leary*:

> He died; *and Father James was brought,*
> *And the Requiem Mass was chanted.*
> The neighbours came; we dug his grave
> Near Eily, Kate, and Mary,
> And there he sleeps his last sweet sleep.
> *God rest you!* Caoch O Leary.

The Course of Irish Verse

I claim nothing for such lines but that they are Catholic: better poets were not simple enough to tell so naturally what happened when an Irish Catholic died. The tinge is in a better poem than *Caoch*: *Bouchaleen Bawn*: in which the theme of Catholic religion conflicting with fairy magic, and expressed in something like peasant speech, makes a composition of originality whose elements were later to work more tellingly:

The pulse of my heart was my Bouchaleen Bawn;
The light of my eyes was my Bouchaleen Bawn.
From Dinan's red wave to the tower of Kilvawn,
You'd not meet the like of my Bouchaleen Bawn!

But, Christ save the hearers! his angel forsook him—
My curse on the queen of the fairies—she took him—
Last All-hallow's eve as he came by Knockbawn,
She saw—loved, and 'struck' my poor Bouchaleen Bawn,

I said to myself, sure it cannot be harm,
To go to the wise man, and ask for a charm;
'Twill cost but a crown, and my heart's blood I'd pawn,
To purchase from bondage my Bouchaleen Bawn.

I went to the priest, and he spoke about heaven;
And said that my failings would not be forgiven,
If ever I'd cross the gray fairy-man's bawn;
Or try my weird spells for my Bouchaleen Bawn.

I'll take his advice, though God knows my heart's breaking;
I start in my sleep, and I weep when I'm waking.
O I long for the blush of eternity's dawn,
When again I shall meet my own Bouchaleen Bawn.

Seven years of literary spy-work in Radio Éireann and the Abbey Theatre have taught me much about underground trends in literature, including this fact: that writers who are unsuccessful and unsophisticated do often, through unspoiled innocence, tend strongly towards good but unpopular aims, though they fail to reach them wholly. The right idea does not always occur at first to the right person, the one who can realise it; and those I speak of are failing (which is the point) *not* to do the things the dominant writers are doing, but to do quite different things; and often they are weak-tongued prophets of what next will predominate. Keegan was just such a writer.

His talent was weak, but his world was one; he was an Irish countryman living with his kind, schooled beside and by them, accepting their creed at precisely their level, and adept as they in the cults and the formulae of old superstitions which were tangled into their creed. By dint of talent and superior knowledge of English, he was more articulate than they; hence he was a chink through which something of their lives could stare, like a prisoner's eye. Of the poets of his time who, as poets, could have bought and sold John Keegan, few composed poems more warmly Irish than his, though they wrote *better* poems, absolutely speaking. That *Christ save the hearers* is the Gael's eye staring through the English wall—the sort of immediate translation which Hyde later turned to a principle.

If most of the Catholic poets failed to write like Keegan, and if those others also failed, who, through refined sen-

sibility, approached the common Irish, have no doubt in
the world that the Donnybrook Fair reciters were im-
mured against his achievement.

I must not draw out this thread too far. I was speaking
of the general weaving of Irish themes into English writing; let me summarise what so far had taken place.

History came in first, because history was first translated—of prose, that is; and because history was the matter closest to political nationalism, the sort first learnt by
the Anglo-Irish. Mythology *began* to come in early: Charlotte Brooke, the pioneer translator, wrote a poem of her
own on the coming of the Iron Age to Ireland; yet, so far
as I know, mythology did not properly enter our verse in
English till decades afterwards, when Moore wrote songs
of the Children of Lir and The Sons of Uisneach, and
Ferguson wrote *Déirdre, The Quest of the Táin, Conary*
and so forth.

From mythology and history to patriotic sentiment was
an easy step; there came poems on Ireland as an ideal
being, and on Irish places; laments for the newly-dead;
aspirations after liberty and unity, and much of that sort.
As everyone knows, Moore was among the first to write
these, too, and he wrote them better than others; but
there were others, and by the time of the *Nation* their
name was Legion.

The theme of faery and magic is distinct from that of
mythology, and this theme peeped out early also, the Age

of Reason being over. As we should expect, it did not first allure the sophisticated poets. Luke Aylmer Connolly's *Enchanted Island* is a reasonably haunted place, as is the churchyard in Carleton's *Sir Turlough;* but Lover's *Fairy Boy* is talk about, not from, the other world, and Griffin's *Hy Brasail* is dismally unethereal. The transporting breath is, however, in Keegan's *Bouchaleen Bawn,* and in Ferguson, as I said already.

Ferguson, we may note, is clearly a poet who binds these developments together; but before giving him his due regard I must revert to progress on the side of form, feeling, mode and mood.

V

AFTER THOMAS MOORE THE NEXT VITAL POET IS CALLA-nan (1795-1829) akin both to Moore and to Keegan. His gift and schooling were nearer Moore's, his soil and water nearer Keegan's. Moore was happy and Keegan was happy; Moore because, mentally as well as bodily, he slid with ease from Ireland to London, Keegan because he was earthed in Ireland. Callanan missed happiness because he slid both ways, drawn to the right by his own community, drawn to the left by the lettered English town. But then most of the Catholic poets of the nineteenth century have Callanan's ragged-minded look: Walsh, even Mangan, Griffin most certainly, and Denis Florence MacCarthy for sure. Moore escaped it, but paid for escaping; he is complete, professional, but "thin." It was a malady of maladjustment, a fight between mind and *milieu*. The Protestant poets—Ferguson, Allingham and Yeats are examples—had another type of incompleteness, but it did not maim them so visibly.

Callanan might not have been unhappy had he not, without thinking, taken Irish life seriously, in the way Moore did in his *Irish Melodies*. He was inside Irish life, and it did not seem to him a Donnybrook Fair. He did not *decide* to find gravity within that life; he probably did not decide anything about it, one way or another; he just was of that life and could not treat it as an outside entertainment got up specially for him. He can scarcely have realised how new that position was, among our English-writing poets. His gravity is not to be confused with his Byronic gloom, for that of course was a young poet's plagiarism. Look for the gravity in his version of O Gnive's *Lament*:

> How dimm'd is the glory that circled the Gael,
> And fall'n the high people of green Innisfail!
>
> We know not our country, so strange is her face,
> Her sons once her glory are now her disgrace.
> Gone, gone is the beauty of fair Innisfail,
> For the stranger now rules in the land of the Gael.

Not alone is this a grave, strong speech, different to the whiskey giggle of Handy Andy, but it swells a diaphragm lacking in the poems of the *Nation*, Davis' *La-*

ment for Owen Roe O'Neill alone excepted. To be sure it is a shade rhetorical; but to find it like Lionel Johnson is to measure it well, and by no means to dispraise it.

Callanan did better than this. *O say, my brown Drimin* and *The Outlaw of Loch Lene* are poems we split no hairs about, but praise at once, declaring them good and Irish and specifying their qualities. *Brown Drimin* has that marriage of matter with unstopped melody which makes the lyric, and the *Outlaw* is at first hearing detectably un-English. Prosody in England had had many victories, but this particular marshalling and marching of sounds had not occurred there; it came clean out of Irish, and to the present day few but Irish poets make it happen in verse in English.

> O many a day have I made good ale in the glen,
> That came not of stream or malt—like the brewing of
>   men!
> My bed was the ground; my roof, the greenwood above,
> And the wealth that I sought, one far kind glance from my
>   love.

Quiller-Couch seized on the last phrase of this lyric to describe its like in our poetry. The phrase is: "The sweet, wild twist of her song." So Callanan named the quality he had.

This Cork poet published only one book, and in it there are about a hundred small pages. Not more than eight or nine pieces in it are of any poetic value, so it may seem odd that Irish critics seldom fail to allude to their author, when discussing the course of our poetry in English. The reason is simple. His historical importance is considerable, and arises from the novelty of finding in his translations from Gaelic poetry the latter's hitherto uncaught, but in Callanan undeniable, cadence.

What happened was this: a genuine poet was born in such a place, of such people, and with such a disposition, that he sought the society of Irish-speaking Munster-folk, and, knowing and loving them and their region, got (half-unconsciously perhaps) a dash of their colour into English when translating their poems. It did not happen that any previous translator carried all the passes; so it did not happen that any before him, except Moore in three or four songs, did what he did.

That is why we count him important. He began the victories.

VI

WE COME BACK TO SAMUEL FERGUSON (1810-1886), Belfastman.

He bound together, as I already have said, and as great talents frequently do, much that had been hesitantly originated before him. He was a born poet; a scholar in several departments; a patriot, though not a separatist; a religious, though not a Catholic, man. He wrote ballads, plays, lyrics and epics on Irish history, myth and fairy-

tale; the roads, rivers and fields of Ireland made most of
his verse; and to-day he is still an eminent translator of
Gaelic poetry. His translations are poems, yet literal in
high degree, a success very rarely achieved before him;
and he added a third achievement, by coming close in
some of his versions to the gait of his originals. These have
held their place in all the anthologies, and should some
new book of our verse be made to-morrow, it would need
to include some poems from his hand—*Pastheen Finn,
The Coolun, Cashel of Munster, Ceann Dubh Dilis, The
Fair Hills of Holy Ireland,* these would probably be among
them. Here is a snatch from *Cashel of Munster*:

> I'll wed you without herds, without money, or rich array,
> And I'll wed you on a dewy morning at day-dawn grey;
> My bitter woe it is, love, that we are not far away,
> In Cashel town, though the bare deal board were our
> marriage-bed this day!

He nowhere mentions Callanan, but here he has the
long, wavering line which *The Outlaw of Loch Lene* first
brought into our translations, and which is one of the most
certifiable additions we have made to prosody in English.
Yeats was to catch its charm and develop it.

In one of his original poems—*The Fairy Thorn*—he
far surpassed Keegan in the latter's special effect: "glam-
ourie." It is a lyric of high worth, on any count; dyed in
the *dayli'gone.* One never forgets it, once having felt its
fineness: a poem to be named with Allingham's *Up the*

The Course of Irish Verse

Airy Mountain, Yeats's *The Stolen Child* and O Rahilly's
Gile na Gile. Those who find Ferguson prosy should have
it read to them. Our immediate concern with it here is its
use of internal assonance.

> Get up, our Anna *dear,* from the *weary* spinning *wheel;*
> For your father's on the hill, and your mother is asleep;
> Come up above the *crags,* and we'll *dance* a Highland reel
> Around the Fairy Thorn on the steep.

> At Anna *Grace's* door 'twas thus the *maidens* cried,
> Three merry *maidens fair* in kirtles of the green;
> And Anna *laid* the rock and the *weary wheel* aside,
> The *fairest* of the four, I ween.

> They're glancing through the glimmer of the quiet eve,
> Away in milky *wavings* of neck and ankle *bare;*
> The heavy-sliding *stream* in its *sleepy* song they *leave,*
> And the crags in the ghostly air.

This device he learned, of course, from his Gaelic poets,
with whom it is beloved, and it prints the Gaelic mark
indelibly on his lovely poem.

His lyrics—those I have named, and others like *Mes-
gedra, The Welshmen of Tirawley, The Forging of the
Anchor,* and *Déirdre's Lament for the Sons of Uisneach,*
are more admired nowadays than are his epical *Conary,
Congal* or *Quest of the Táin,* or his play, *Déirdre;* and
probably that as a judgment is sound enough; the lyrics remain fresh and pleasing after all the poets who have written since, while the intervening verse has made the epics
seem a little bald and long-drawn. Not that they are by

25

any means unreadable or without virtue; but he did not forge an epic, as he did a lyric, instrument; he could not resist the form and pressure of the great narrative verse of England in his time; and the Irish names, characters and places of his poems do not induce an Irish style.

It would be easy, notwithstanding, to over-censure his long poems. They are poetry in a respectable degree, and he did stout service to our literature in writing them. It was an independent mind which chose, at that point of time, to take as epical themes the myths of a people other than the Greeks and Romans. It is true the shady Mac-Pherson had fluttered the Celtic fringe in the eyes of the lettered world; it is true also that the Scandinavian fogs had been blown aside a piece—Thomas Gray, for all he was a classicist, had taken short walks towards both Wales and the Northland; but it is equally true that Gaelic mythology—accurate Gaelic mythology, especially—was still an outland, and not to be tilled by respectable, scholarly Protestant poets. Ferguson tilled it, decades before Standish O Grady and the language revival. Our hearts warm to the sturdy patriot and poet. We are glad Yeats praised him, even if the terms of some of his praise are no longer allowable.

Two quotations to end this note; the first an expression, remarkable in its day as coming from the Ascendancy, of desire to take Irish history and Irish tradition as the hinterland of the life of the Irish-born; the second an example of the stateliness and grave melody which Ferguson could give to his translations from the Irish:

For, thou, for them, alas! nor History hast
    Nor even Tradition; and the Man aspires
To link his present with his country's past,
    And live anew in knowledge of his sires;
No rootless colonist of an alien earth,
    Proud but of patient lungs and pliant limb,
A stranger in the land that gave him birth,
    The land a stranger to itself and him.
              (From *Mesgedra*)

•

The lions of the hill are gone,
And I am left alone—alone—
Dig the grave both wide and deep,
For I am sick and fain would sleep!

The falcons of the wood are flown,
And I am left—alone—alone—
Dig the grave both deep and wide,
And let us slumber side by side.

The dragons of the rock are sleeping,
Sleep that wakes not for our weeping:
Dig the grave and make it ready;
Lay me on my true-love's body.

•

Oh! to hear my true Love singing,
Sweet as sounds of trumpets ringing:
Like the sway of ocean swelling
Roll'd his deep voice round our dwelling.

Oh! to hear the echoes pealing
Round our green and fairy sheeling,
When the Three, with soaring chorus,
Pass'd the silent skylark o'er us.

27

Echo now, sleep, morn and even—
Lark alone enchant the heaven!—
Ardan's lips are scant of breath,—
Nessa's tongue is cold in death.

(From *Déirdre's Lament for the Sons of Uisneach*.)

VII

BEFORE TAKING UP THE CONSIDERATION OF AN EVEN
more considerable poet than Ferguson I must touch on the
verse of another minor but historically important one,
Edward Walsh of Cork (1805-1850).

Walsh, in a way, was a better-schooled John Keegan;
education did not partly spoil him, as it partly spoiled
Callanan; but then Callanan was something of a creator,
Walsh a translator almost wholly. He (Walsh) was, anyhow, John Keegan in his verse, and Thomas Davis in his
fervent politics. I called him in an ampler essay the one
fully-orbed Irishman of his day: a Catholic; educated;
at one with the peasants except in their limitations; a
lover of spoken Irish and of its music, poetry and history;
a separatist and all but a martyr; a man so poor and
denied that he coveted Mitchel's deportation to Botany
Bay. He failed of Keegan's intuition that countrymen's
English was poetical speech—perhaps because he was
a schoolmaster, perhaps because the countrymen he felt
most for spoke Irish; and he was less the impression-
able poet than Callanan, therefore the less detachable

from English sing-song in metre. Nevertheless, he did not petrify the verses he translated, as the team of John Hardiman did in their massive anthology; his versions are, the most of them, alive, he uses Gaelic names and refrains in them, and he footed once or twice that mazy and graceful curve on which Ferguson and Callanan had danced.

He is remembered as Callanan is, as one who tipped our verse in the way that would lead it to distinction. But Walsh did it consciously, as part of a fervent belief. He appreciated several of the formal virtues of his originals, determined to reproduce them in translating, and did, in fact, do this thing, in a certain degree. That is, he fits the words always to the tune, as Moore did, arriving as did Moore, Callanan and Ferguson at the long, sinuous line; and he "vowels" well, employing cross-rhyme and assonance. His chief fault was a stiff, often bookish diction; the source of his considerable influence, his relative faithfulness and the completeness, in a given genre—that of Jacobite poetry—of what he attempted.

A stanza from his best poem, *Have you been at Carrick*, will show his quality:

Have you been at Carrick, and saw you my true-love there?
And saw you her features, all beautiful, bright and fair?
Saw you the most fragrant, flowering sweet apple-tree?—
O! saw you my lov'd one, and pines she in grief like me?

VIII

THE NEXT NAME WE MUST NAME IS JAMES CLARENCE Mangan's (1803-1849); a name as yet, or so it seems to me, not sufficiently famous. For, taken simply as a poet he is more than good; while, taken as an Irish poet he is first for three quarters of his century.

He had, no doubt of it at all, a signal poetic equipment, which we might in a way sum-up as acrobatic agility of mind—though the phrase only half-includes his deep, if florid, feeling. The outward mark of his agility, as one might surmise, is flexible and venturesome technique; while his range of themes, his zest that never flagged, his gaiety, his interest in languages and literatures, and finally his high and unconventional estimate of Gaelic poetry— these are more inward signs. Admitting all the blotches on his sometimes half-formed work, and contrasting with the high-polished art of a Yeats his frequent slapdashness, one must nonetheless say that only a poet of major dimensions could have done what this Mangan did in his period and circumstance. Had he lived when the pollen of poetry was denser in the air of Ireland, he would have been, without "only" or "if," without "but" or "perhaps," a major poet. Or so I read him.

His technique was surely remarkable. He seldom re-used a metre or a stanzaic form; he cast new shapes for his stanzas, and (in Saintsbury's phrase) "fingered" his metres personally; he was a virtuoso in euphony, a master of sonorous eloquence, and involved his vowel and con-

sonant with fine effect. He had that indubitable mark of
the excellent lyrist: the faculty for varying line-lengths
within the stanza; that other mark: the consummate
handling of refrain. Proper names in his poems were often
used with grandeur; he could give to his lines the climate
of the country of his theme; and finally, a decisive mark
of his many-sidedness: his verses crawled or walked or
sped at his need.

To make evident his metrical fineness and diversity one
need not draw upon any but the well-known poems. There
are these among the versions from the Irish: *The Woman
of Three Cows; O Hussey's Ode to the Maguire; Dark
Rosaleen; Kathaleen Ny Houlihan; O Woman of the
Piercing Wail; St. Patrick's Hymn before Tara; The
Lamentation of Mac Liag;* and *Lift up the Drooping
Head.* Among the orginal poems there are these: *A Vision
of Connacht; The Time of the Barmecides; The Nameless
One; The Karamanian Exile* and *Solomon, Where is thy
throne?*
There, then, are thirteen of his choicest poems; no two
identical in basic metrical line; no two identical in group-
ing of lines; no two which do not differ in their schemes
of rhyming; hardly a pair with the same kind of subject
or mood; and scarcely one with a debt particular to any
poet writing in English. Their originality is obvious; but
more, it is organic, bound-up with the effects intended
and achieving those effects.
From which shall I quote? Not from *Dark Rosaleen*:

for all of us have it on our ears, and most on our tongues as well. *O Hussey's Ode to the Maguire* shall give us a stanza:

> Though he were even a wolf ranging the round green woods,
> Though he were even a pleasant salmon in the unchainable sea,
> Though he were a wild mountain eagle, he could scarce bear, he,
> This sharp, sore sleet, these howling floods.

Where did Mangan get that freedom from the current sing-song, that spacious handling, that sureness in newness? It recalls the breakaway of Moore: *At the mid hour of night.* But the source of Moore's moment of Gaelic quality we know to have been the tunes to which he was writing; while Mangan, we know, was not writing to a tune, and his metre is other than that of the Gaelic poem. Furthermore, Moore broke away only four or five times; while Mangan did it quite often.

Then there is *Woman of Three Cows.* We all, of course, know it well, but mainly for its humour; if someone who believes in such questions were suddenly to ask us "Quote for me a great single line from an Irish poet"—would we think of turning to these verses? Yet listen to this:

> O think of Donnell of the ships, the Chief whom nothing daunted—
> See how he fell in distant Spain, unchronicled, unchaunted!

He sleeps, the great O Sullivan, where thunder cannot
  rouse—
Then ask yourself, should you be proud, good Woman of
  Three Cows!

I find that third line time after time reverberating in
memory.—But I was speaking of *metrical* virtue, and the
virtue of that line is more in euphony than narrowly in
metre—though, by the same token, I could make it exemplify metrical skill, by contrasting the fling and the
fall of its syllables with the fall and the fling of the other
third lines of the poem.

But there *is* a purely metrical trait in the poem, which
might not be detected before the twentieth scrutiny. It is
this: that the first and second lines of every quatrain finish on a weak syllable, while the third and fourth finish
on a strong one, every time. The effect when observed is
quite strange, and not easily described. I think I might say
at least this: that Gaelic poetry favours the unstressed
line-ending, a shade or two more than does English poetry;
therefore, the use of it in versions from the Irish gives
them a Gaelic footstep. Mangan's wary ear, however,
warned him of the risk of employing this ending in *every*
line: had he done so the stanza would appear to be pitch-
ing headlong; while its use in only the first two lines gives
these momentum, and the strong-stressed endings of the
second two lines "ramp" each stanza stoutly.

Kathaleen-ny-Houlihan again shows cause for admiration of Mangan as a metrist. His metre here is a form of

the old "fourteener"—used for great splendour by supple-wristed verse-men, but also by botchers for *plod-plod*: being equally full of perils and of marvellous chances. Mangan did not botch; his wrists responded like an angler's playing a salmon. It is something to his credit, to begin, that, without any forcing, he stresses the opening syllable in all his lines. This is not easy in English. But more to be noted is the fine positioning of pauses, with wide variety of phrase-lengths; sometimes two lines march without halt; sometimes his every step has a check coming after it; sometimes again a half-line, or a whole one, walks at a time. To demonstrate all this properly would take us over-long; here is a single quatrain:

> Sweet and mild would look her face, O none so sweet and
>   mild,
> Could she crush the foes by whom her beauty is reviled;
> Woollen plaids would grace herself and robes of silk her
>   child,
> If the King's son were living here with Kathaleen-ny-Houli-
>   han.

What a stride in that third line; and how finely the fourth one steps, Irish in every motion.

I have pointed only to moderately obvious effects, since I need to exemplify them rapidly; but those who have ears for these things can find more complexity. All such will remark, for example, his touch with refrains. We average poets can stitch our refrains to the hems of stanzas; not all, however, can make them good refrains; nor even the refrains which are good can we stitch *through* stanzas, always knowing just where, and exactly how often, and with what little changes of stitch we ought to place them. Mangan knew. His *Dark Rosaleen* is a classical example.

Among many examples of Mangan's *eloquence*, possibly the chief one is *Gone in the Wind*.

Solomon! where is thy throne? It is gone in the wind.
Babylon! where is thy might? It is gone in the wind.
Like the swift shadows of Noon, like the dreams of the
   Blind
Vanish the glories and pomps of the earth in the wind.

Solomon! where is thy throne? It is gone in the wind.
Babylon! where is thy might? It is gone in the wind.
All that the genius of Man hath achieved or designed
Waits but its hour to be dealt with as dust by the wind.

The scriptures tell us how the Ten Tribes of Israel divided, stood upon opposite hilltops, and spoke The Law across the valley, pinnacle to pinnacle. I hear these anti-phonal queryings and answerings of Mangan's poem, spoken by a double choir in an echoing hall; with the whole choir joining in the third and fourth lines for full-est resonance.

This language of open vowels and flying echoes was often at Mangan's call:

Then I saw thrones,
　　And circling fires,
And a dome rose near me, as by a spell,
　　Whence flowed the tones
　　　Of silver lyres,
And many voices in wreathéd swell;
　　And their thrilling chime
　　　Fell on mine ears
As the heavenly hymn of an angel-band—
　　'It is now the time,
　　　These be the years,
Of Cahal Mor of the Wine-red Hand.'

One notes in him that liquid ease which was Moore's
best quality. Later Irish poets have avoided the facilities
of lesser English verse; they have refined upon its rhythms
and its diction, enlarged the resources of their imagery,
and made their palettes more fit for the nuances of Irish
light and Irish feeling. They have shared, too, in an effort
of contemporary poetry—the working of the cadences of
speech as against those of song. Indeed, in the last few years
some of them, one thinks, incline to *over*work speech
rhythms, incline to be unaware that the lack of singing in
poetry may be more than a technical want. It so often
means that the seed of experience has stopped at the top-
soil of their minds, not penetrated to the deeper earth.
To put it otherwise, their words lack dance and song because the theme in their hearts and minds lacks dance and
song. They are *talking-about* experience, *referring to* it,
indicating it; not, in organised movement and tone and

figure of words, delivering it sensuously, a *livingness* still, but with a separate existence. Now Mangan's poems always dance and sing, and they do so because he has worked them to the state of dance and of song, not because he has tricked them out with jingly rhythms. He avoids the imposture of the borrowed melody and dance-step, and the further imposture of song at the cost of meaning. A reasonable test is his *Time of the Barmecides;* there is nothing very novel in the metre, and the full-blown romanticism of subject and "properties" may jar upon many of his readers; nonetheless, as a sample of its type, it quite certainly succeeds: a handful of Oriental names, another of Oriental words, a detail or two of suggestion—and there is a poem which temperament or theory will scarcely prevent us from liking. Lest we in contemporary Ireland should press his Romanticism overharshly against him, it is well to recall the Byzantine poems of Yeats, and to consider whether, in the matter of exotic symbols and vocabulary, the two Romantics differ in marked degree. A.E. was a third such Romantic.

> I see rich Bagdad once again,
> With its turrets of Moorish mould,
> And the Khalif's twice five hundred men,
> Whose binishes flamed with gold;
> I call up many a gorgeous show—
> Which the pall of Oblivion hides—
> All passed like snow, long, long ago,
> With the time of the Barmecides;
> All passed like snow, long, long ago,
> With the time of the Barmecides.

The Course of Irish Verse

If this were all of Mangan, had he found to engage him nothing but this story-book East, we might talk of exoticism, sickly nostalgia, Turkish Delight Escapism; but it was not all: it was one aspect only, and helps to manifest his many-sidedness.

The emotional, eloquent and opulently-imaged side of Mangan's poetry is incontestably his larger and his better side; it coheres with his character, which is that of the typical Romantic—poverty, alcohol, opium, the habits of the solitary, fervour in religion—and has led us to think solely of his work as sad and sonorous; we forget that he has gusto as well as grandiosity, and not only gusto but gaiety. Doubtless his humorous poems have small worth in themselves, with one or two exceptions; but they show his unending joy in the athletics of rhythm, and, probably, kept him fit for such ceremonial dances as *The ride round the parapet*. Here is its mazy metre:

> She doffed her silks and pearls, and donned instead her
>   hunting-gear,
>   The Lady Eleanora von Alleyne,
> She doffed her silks and pearls, and donned instead her
>   hunting-gear,
> And, till Summer-time was over, as a huntress and a rover,
>   Did she couch upon the mountain and the plain,
>   She, the Lady Eleanora,
>   Noble Lady Eleanora von Alleyne.

(Note the inlay of assonance and internal rhyme.)

The Course of Irish Verse

Such poems as this were in part made possible by his patter-song foolery; contrariwise, the lush romanticism of many of the "versions and perversions" from the German and the Oriental languages finds an analogue in the extravagance of *To the Ingleeze Khafir,* and *The King of the Franks;* though, to qualify still further, this very extravagance is Irish also: it is not the grin of Gay, or the modish smile of Prior which Mangan prefers, but the comical squawk of MacConglinne.

> I hate thee, Djaun Bool,
> Worse than Marid or Afrit,
> Or corpse-eating Ghoul!
> I hate thee like sin,
> From thy mop-head of hair,
> Thy snub-nose and bald chin,
> And thy turkey-cock air;
> Thou vile Ferindjee!
> That thou thus shouldst disturb an
> Old Moslem like me,
> With my Khizzilbash turban,
> Old fogy like me
> With my Khizzilbash turban.

I do not remember whether, in his hunt for anticipations of "The Irish Mode," Ernest Boyd has classified Mangan's extravagance as one; properly he would have so done, for this trait is as certainly racial as the veering flute-breath of Moore's *At the Mid Hour of Night,* or the fey-gay treble of Allingham's *Up the Airy Mountain.* It is

39

doubtful if the point was taken by any of the "Renaissance" poets before James Stephens; so it is one more count for Mangan that he discovered this connaturality with MacConglinne, O Bruadair and the rest.

I spoke a while ago of Mangan's high estimate of Gaelic verse. It is to be reckoned to his credit that he spent the best of his gifts on translating it. Perhaps only Ferguson and Callanan before him had made translations which were certain poetry; and, all things said, he was Ferguson's master. He came a little nearer than anyone before him to preserving his originals' formal elements, though he did not attempt completeness of this kind. We are all his beneficiaries, did he never pen an original line of his own.

Of course he penned many. He wrote too much, and at times wrote windily, at other times wrote with great negligence; but thirty or forty of his pieces, chosen with judgment and taken together, make surely the best block of Anglo-Irish verse by any single writer before the advent of Yeats. "Here", said Lionel Johnson of *Dark Rosaleen,* and I stretch the application of his words, "Here is the chivalry of a nation's faith struck of a sudden into the immortality of music."

Nothing that Mangan gave the translation movement was of greater value than his name; for, once a poet so worthy and engaging had bent *con amore* over Gaelic rhymes, there could never again be doubt of the value of such work. The work repaid him too; it prevented the balloon of Romanticism from hoisting him to a heaven of rainbow-and-vapour dreams. That is to say, it made him an Irish poet; the best sort, poetically speaking, that an Irish poet can be. It gave him the stuff, and much of the shape of some of his finest poems, for example *Dark Rosaleen, Woman of Three Cows* and *O Hussey's Ode to the Maguire*. The second is possibly the clearest proof of how he was enabled to keep his heels from hoisting. Humour was innate in him, but not dry realism; *that* he might have missed had he not translated; his humour, left alone, ran to giddy whimsicality.

Moore might have founded Irish poetry in English, but English admiration and money drew him off such a venture. English unawareness of Mangan, and Mangan's indifference to English judgment, between them held him for Irish poetry; but this holding was, besides, a triumph for the pioneer translators: had *they* not cut the road *he* might not have walked it. Yeats is another who was held, in part, by work less good than his own. The fixed direction of the work of a vital poet at some time hangs by threads, and by these same threads hangs his nation's treasury of poetry.

Yet the talk and behaviour of living men is a palmary influence, and Mangan felt it in the *Nation* group; their propaganda reached him, especially that finest part of their propaganda: the high, bright soul of Thomas Davis. The purseless pioneering scholars with whom he worked

in the Office of the Ordnance Survey, these and John O
Daly the publisher affected him too. For if, as tasters of
verse, we make faces at the rhymes of the *Nation,* we must
think at once of how generous they were to Mangan. He
was poor, eccentric, vexatious, and he sometimes sold
them bad verse; yet they helped him. With their pens they
put back the clock of Irish poetry; with their gentle gen-
erosity to Mangan put it forward again.

Their own abundant verse was rhymed pamphleteer-
ing: political ideas, and crude, easy but ardent emotion
was its Irish side, while diction, metre and the rest were
shoddy English. Davis (now and then) aside, they did
not write poetry. An odd song did not spoil the Irish tunes
to which they wrote; and note that they did write songs
to Irish tunes, emulating Moore. Note, too, their demand
that Gaelic words be rightly spelt. Note finally their finding a place for the artist in their programme.

The *Nation* group indirectly aided the translation
movement, and helped it to affect original poetry. Literary growths are slow: we must not wonder that men do
this and leave that undone in such affairs. Parts come together if a race have luck.

Besides we might say that the *Nation,* by treating verse
so commonly, made it more common, in the sense of more
diffused. They said we required a corpus of Irish songs,
and they tried to write them. They saw that Irish history
was full of good themes, and they tried to treat them. And,
even if their songs and poems were mostly bad, nevertheless they made this much difference: that after their time

it could no longer look queer or provincial to write new poems on Irish historical themes. They stirred the soil, and, later, better farmers grew better crops.

IX

THERE WAS BEGINNING TO BE AN AIR IN ENGLISH-SPEAKing Ireland, an air a little like that in which Irish was alive. The Irish writer knew by now he had a country of his own, which was, in the phrase of the love-song, lovely to look at, delightful to know. He knew it had a long history, even an old literature; that some people actually held it could rule itself; that, whatever about such far-fetched notions as the last, Ireland was assuredly picturesque, as witness its vivid mythology; that Catholics might, to a tolerant man, appear to have been roughly treated, worthy of a shade more forbearance—and so on. The air became a breath more tangible when Miss Maria Edgeworth—a novelist sufficiently good to give hints to Sir Walter Scott—arose among the Ascendancy, and, in all seriousness, wrote contemporary and historical, but always successful stories of the Irish. It began to thicken decidedly when the common run of the Irish threw up a story-teller, a man reared on a small farm who talked Irish through most of his youth and doggedly butted his way to that other culture of Latin and English. He prejudiced the matter a bit by writing proselytising tracts; but he wrote his stories—however awkwardly—from inside a small farmer's cottage. His stories were grave as well as humorous; he even had tragedies about peasants—their famines and so on; and he seemed to write something like the bastard English they spoke themselves. His books, impossibly, were read, and perhaps were even good. The air prevailed.

There were learned societies too, growing, researching, publishing. There were land agitations, and the Catholic Church emerging from behind the Mass-Rock. Bishops and priests in full view, and churches of stone going up. And this . . . and that . . .

X

AUBREY DE VERE (1814-1902), BY EARLY ENVIRONMENT, by make of mind and heart, and by length of life, was such a man as should perceive this atmosphere. Of County Limerick stock and born there; son and brother to poets and himself a poet; a sensitive, religious, philosophical man, who changed his religion through conviction, and thereafter lived and made poems like a Catholic; he lived, as the dates show, from the first quarter of one century to the opening years of the next (so that the friend of Wordsworth all but saw Yeats's middle-age); and, to end this summary, he worked, as the records tell, to blunt the teeth of hunger among the poor. In company, Sir William Wilde, the father of Oscar, introduced him as "my Papist friend."

44

The Course of Irish Verse

Perhaps this quoted phrase explains in part why the Irish atmosphere to which de Vere should have been more sensitive did not, in fact, Irishise his work. The Catholic poet—even the gentleman convert—was still unhelped by the cultural *milieu*. There were still two atmospheres, and the older resisted the new; the moulds made long before were hard to break.

De Vere the poet was formed by his earlier years, perhaps chiefly by his friendship with Wordsworth—a potent influence indeed for a minor poet; and that, I surmise, is why I think of him as early nineteenth century, though most of his work was done in the second half: one does not see Mangan, Ferguson and Callanan, or the interest in Irish affecting him. Of course he wrote much on Irish history, and, after his conversion, on Catholic history and belief; but, except in a handful of poems, not in an Irish way. Such waste among Irish poets: they were mentally transplanted. His *Innisfail* and *Legends of Saint Patrick* might conceivably have held against the moths were they spun of Irish threads; as it is they are holes all over. The matter, again, may be simpler: that he lacked great force; and certainly his watery gentility thinned most that he made; yet a lyric here 'and there authorises speculation. I am thinking, of course, of *The Little Black Rose, The Wedding of the Clans* and *The Dirge of Rory O More*. Strange (have I said it before?) how such as de Vere remain in none but their *Irish* poems. Is it true of other nations? . . . I quote *The Little Black Rose*:

The little Black Rose shall be red at last!
What made it black but the East wind dry,
And the tear of the widow that fell on it fast?
It shall redden the hills when June is nigh!

The Silk of the Kine shall rest at last!
What drave her forth but the dragon-fly?
In the golden vale she shall feed full fast
With her mild gold horn, and her slow dark eye.

The wounded wood-dove lies dead at last:
The pine, long bleeding, it shall not die!
—This song is secret. Mine ear it passed
In a wind o'er the plains of Athenry.

XI

DENIS FLORENCE MAC CARTHY (1817-1882) WAS VERY like de Vere, but his gift was even less, and the Gaelic finger more entirely failed to mark him. He was one of those vexatious Irishmen, cultural emigrés, who went versioning the divers dialects of Europe and Asia while an older poetry than most wanted service at home. Edward Fitzgerald, Thomas Anster, "Father Prout" and so on. May they rest where they are; let us throttle the yells of disgust which we long—how strenuously—to loose upon their spirits over this world's edge. . . I do not know a couplet of MacCarthy's, whether he or Calderon first inked it, that would make us turn a page to read on an idle day. It is the doom of poets who do not dig their own earth. Let us dig . . .

WILLIAM ALLINGHAM (1824-1889) WAS DIFFERENT FROM these. First he had a livelier vein, and one reckons him with Ferguson and Mangan and Moore, as a poet *pur sang*. Better, perhaps, say with Moore and Darley, since he lived so much in England; yet he guessed his way much better than Darley to "the secret song". He even guessed better than Moore, we might say. In a very few years we will, more than at present, read him and write of him.

In an essay on Allingham in *Irish Literary and Musical Studies,* Alfred Perceval Graves has some first-hand facts, supplied by a cousin of Allingham and supplemented from Graves's own acquaintance with the poet. Of these some are relevant here, but they must be condensed. They show that his Irish element had these three sources: ballads he heard sung in Donegal; his study of the troubles about land in Ireland; and his study of Gaelic literature.

Goldsmith projected his songs into Dublin streets that they might be sung as he walked unrecognised around. Allingham, it seems, possibly through hearing this of Goldsmith, coveted the same kind of fame without name. He wanted the girls of Donegal who spun by half-doors and sang, to sing his words and not know who made them. He would pick up the ballads they sang already, anonymous, imperfect but racy things, and would improve them; then he would have them printed on blue sheets, with woodcuts, like the ones they were used to; he would circulate

47

these in Ballyshannon, and, surely enough, the girls did sing them and the poet put his head in the air. . . This remodelling of ballad-singers' songs was done long after by Yeats, by Colum and by Joseph Campbell; and some of their best-liked songs were so made, in the embrace of folk-mind with the mind of the cultivated poet. F. R. Higgins, still later, liked making songs in this way.

Allingham identifies five of these ballads of his—or rather of his remodelling—which the Donegal girls sang. They are: *The Milkmaid; Lovely Mary Donnelly; The Girl's Lamentation; Nanny's Sailor Lad,* and *The Nobleman's Wedding.*

They are by no means all of a piece. *The Milkmaid* is a pretty song to sing, but pseudo-pastoral and more English than Irish. *Mary Donnelly* has an Irish tune, a ballad's artlessness, Irish country furnishings—rowan tree, blind fiddler, jigs, grass-roofed cottages—despite all which it is almost picture post-card Irish. It is sung in character by Mary's lover, and sounds made-up for the peasants. For instance there is this line:

> The music nearly killed itself to listen to her feet.

Music-hall comics would find this very Irish, but the Irish language couldn't say it without idiomatic suicide. I shall some day say in the Gaeltacht:

> Ba dhóbair don gceol é féin a mharbhú d'iarraidh éisteacht len a coísiní.

48

The Course of Irish Verse

Then slowly I shall sip my stout, looking over the brim at the Gaeltacht men. They will probably take my stout very gently away.

The Girl's Lamentation is "a world elsewhere". I had the luck some years ago to re-introduce this poem to literary Dublin, and well worth doing it was. It seems impossible that Thomas MacDonagh knew it; he would scarcely then have found Allingham wanting in "the Irish accent of Ferguson". It is a good poem and historically notable. I am no bibliographer, but, stumbling by pure chance on the 1877 Boston edition of *Songs, Ballads and Stories,* and finding the poem there, I was surprised that my betters had missed it. It is not in the anthologies, not even in Pádraic Colum's, and this is strange, because Colum in particular should have pounced on it, he himself having translated and paraphrased some *Love-Songs of Connacht,* which *The Girl's Lamentation* resembles. Rosetti thought the poem *most admirable,* thereby showing power to value what must have been strange to him.

It is seventy-two lines long, too many for these pages. Here are twenty.

> With grief and mourning I sit to spin;
> My love pass'd by, and he didn't come in;
> He passes by me, both day and night,
> And carries off my poor heart's delight.
>
> There is a tavern in yonder town,
> My love goes there and he spends a crown,
> He takes a strange girl upon his knee,
> And never more gives a thought to me.

49

Says he "We'll wed without loss of time,
And sure our love's but a little crime";
My apron-string now is wearing short,
And my love he seeks other girls to court.

O with him I'd go if I had my will,
I'd follow him barefoot o'er rock and hill;
I'd never once speak of all my grief
If he'd give me a smile for my heart's relief.

•

As through the long lonesome night I lie,
I'd give the world if I might but cry;
But I mustn't moan there or raise my voice,
And the tears run down without any noise.

It is a true, heart-breaking poem, with many marks upon it of a pen (or rather of a tongue: this is speech, not writing) older than Allingham's. Echoes waken after it for those who know Irish balladry: in the second stanza, for example; and they will not need to have *Shule agradh* set by it, or many other folk-songs. Yet Allingham was not the man to find a song and add nothing but his name to it; some of the praise must be his—as much as or more than Yeats has received for *Down by the Salley Gardens,* or Colum for *She moved through the Fair*—and the chief points of praise are, that he ensured its preservation and preserved its simplicity.

Note that these songs are, after remodelling, meant to go back to the clay which made them: the Irish country-folk. Who before Allingham, I mean of his class, would have had such a wish? And the wish affected the modelling: if Donegal spinners were to spin to new versions the wording must be suited; the English must be such at they spoke, or not too unlike it.

This Irish way with English speech troubled Allingham a bit. At first he thought the country-people's English "imperfect and distorted" and the possible choice from it of words fit for poetry "narrowly limited" and "lacking that variety and raciness which is sometimes in the gift of a genuine peculiar dialect." John Keegan used this speech without question, and Carleton had tried it too; but Allingham was possibly the earliest writer of accomplished style and ample culture to ponder its worth. He twice modified his first opinion and in the end allowed that "some not unimportant poetical results might flow from a judicious treatment of Irish dialect." We know that Synge and others agreed, and proved him right.

The story of *The Nobleman's Wedding* is more Border Ballad than Irish, but it goes to an Irish tune and I will venture saying—though I have not tested the opinion— that its sliding movement is not common in English poetry.

> Once I was guest at a Nobleman's wedding;
> Fair was the bride, but she scarce had been kind;
> And now in our mirth she had tears nigh the shedding;
> Her former true lover still runs in her mind.

Graves makes *Adieu to Belashanny* Allingham's masterpiece in this kind; and, with *Up the Airy Mountain,* it is his best-known poem; but I do not like it much: its mechanical metre offends me, though its detail is very Irish, and its feeling tender.

Being intimate with the Pre-Raphaelites (he found Rossetti's wife for him) and being Irish, he of course wrote "magic-poems"; *Up the Airy Mountain* and *The Maids of Elfin-Mere* "translate" us, in Bottom's sense. Being Allingham he made a magic-poem for children, which would "translate" them indeed, but, having translated would also entertain them in an extra manner. I have seen Dublin children dash up Killiney Hill as they chanted it . . . Yeats's *Fairy Child* was "solemn-eyed."

Is it bizarre to see Allingham's innately lyrical mind as another token of his Irishry?

Other races are lyrical, and some have excelled us in lyric verse; but few have a poetry so over-ridingly lyric; the Irish have so insistently doated on passionate singing that they tend to forgo all other poetical glory. . . It is a limitation; and yet lyric verse is surely the ultimate kind, the one total, instantaneous transubstantiation of a spiritual event, the one sort of poetry that in all its words is substantial heat and shine? It may be error and upon me proved, but times there are when philosophic poetry, and even the verse of great drama, seem to me to have failed of the full, to have been what they are for this reason: that the fire of the poet who forged them was under the lyric heat.

Allingham, anyhow, was first and last a lyricist. His victories are lyrics and his failures long narratives, and in that he is not un-Irish. In some of his failures his themes and feelings were Irish, and his knowledge adequate. Had Irish culture had the grip to hold him, or had his own force for inauguration been stronger, he might have preceded Yeats as Master-Builder. His planning should have been sound.

XIII

ALLINGHAM DIED IN 1889, A FEW YEARS AFTER YEATS began to publish, and I think some trace of the older man may be shown in the younger; certainly their having an Irish member would not weaken the Pre-Raphaelites' attraction for Yeats.

Excepting Larminie, of whom I shall speak in a moment, there was no poet of mark between Aubrey de Vere and Allingham on the one side and Yeats on the other; but a man here and a woman there gave each a poem or two of worth. *The Wearin' of the Green* and *The Croppy Boy* continued the ballad line; Robert Dwyer Joyce in *The Drynan Dhun* and elsewhere has the "track of the Gaelic" upon him; Sigerson widened the scope of translation to include our older and middle verse; and Todhunter followed him a couple of paces, pausing long enough to make one of the hall-marked poems: the piercing *Aghadoe*. Spoken well, this poem can bring an Irish audience to tears:

There's a glade in Aghadoe, Aghadoe, Aghadoe,
There's a green and silent glade in Aghadoe,
Where we met, my love and I, love's fair planet in the sky,
O'er that sweet and silent glade in Aghadoe.

There's a glen in Aghadoe, Aghadoe, Aghadoe,
There's a deep and secret glen in Aghadoe,
Where I hid him from the eyes of the redcoats and the spies,
That year the trouble came to Aghadoe.

•

For they tracked me to that glen in Aghadoe, Aghadoe,
When the price was on his head in Aghadoe;
O'er the mountain, through the wood, as I stole to him
with food,
When in hiding lone he lay in Aghadoe.

•

I walked to Mallow Town from Aghadoe, Aghadoe,
Brought his head from the jail's gate to Aghadoe;
Then I covered him with fern, and I piled on him the
cairn,
Like an Irish king he sleeps in Aghadoe.

Cecil Frances Alexander (1825-1895) exemplifies this momentary inbreak of native Irish life, this sea overtopping a dyke and leaving some wrack behind, which accounts for those "poems of the Irish mode" that lie so lonely on the masses of English verse in the work of the de Veres and their like. She wrote one Irish poem.

She and her husband—Protestant Archishop of Armagh —each wrote verse. Some of his has dignity and grave feeling; and she wrote hymns which are still in her

Church's hymnals: *There is a green hill far away* is one well known. She was of English and Anglo-Irish family, but was born and lived in Ireland. Her husband was a Derryman, and the county next his—Donegal—was the only one to tone her work. *The Legend of Stumpie's Brae,* her Irish poem, takes its story from that county, and its language is "the peculiar semi-Scottish dialect spoken in the north of Ireland."

Why did our poets so long leave this individual speech unused in poetry? It is strictly the only dialect in the English of Ireland; for the special savour of the tongue in the rest of our country is not of wholly English origin; it is half at least the Gaelic herb flavouring the English meat; for the rest it is Tudor English, with hints of Norse and of Norman. The North has the only dialect and it pokes through the rest like a bare big toe through a sock. Yet exhaustive anthologies, like Cooke's, and Brooke and Rolleston's, have no early example of its use in verse excepting a feeble song by James McKowen (1814-1889). One Charlotte Nooth did indeed publish some Irish ballads in 1815 which she alleged to be written "in the dialect of the lower Classes of People in the northern Parts of Ireland"; but her dialect is as thin as her poetry. Ferguson has no trace of Northern idiom; Allingham's Irish-English is such as we hear in any part of Ireland; and, ironically, Sigerson, so proud of the things of the North, left the racy Tyrone vernacular out of reach of his pen for a very long lifetime.

The fact is doubly odd; first because the Ulsterman is
very assertive and prone to prize what is his; and second
because Robert Burns, whom Ulstermen claim as a poetical first cousin, sang like a bird in a speech very like
their own.

All this gives to *Stumpie's Brae* a singular interest; but
its strictly poetical interest is also quite big.

It contains one hundred and forty lines, so its next print-
ing must be left, with my compliments, to the next an-
thologist. The story, in a sentence, is this: a peasant and
his wife murder a pedlar; then, finding him literally too
big for his box, sever his legs at the knees; only to find
that, go they where they will, even to the backwoods of
America, there goes Stumpie stumping about them on two
bloody knee-bones:

> And through the door, like a sough of air,
> And stump, stump, round the twa,
> Wi' his bloody head, and his knee banes bare—
> They'd maist ha'e died of awe.

> Still year and day, as the clock struck nine,
> The hour when they did the sin,
> The wee bit dog began to whine,
> And the ghaist came clattering in.

> And stump, stump, stump to his plays again,
> And o'er the stools and chairs;
> Ye'd surely ha'e thought ten women and men
> Were dancing there in pairs.

The ship swam o'er the water clear
Wi' the help o' the eastern breeze;
But the vera first sound in guilty fear,
O'er the wide, smooth deck, that fell on their ear
Was the tapping o' them twa knees.

XIV

WILLIAM LARMINIE (1850-1889), I SAID, WAS THE SINGLE poet of mark between de Vere and Allingham on the one side and Yeats on the other. It was not so much what Larminie composed as what he proposed that makes him notable. He made his proposition in an essay, and followed it in verse; but neither affected other poets' work until Larminie was dead for close on forty years.

Not that the essay was forgotten. The long-remembering A. E., who took out his spiritual seed-bag whenever a new poet appeared, discoursed of Larminie's essay to three generations of versemen. One of them told me so, and they all talked as though they'd read it. Yet the one poet who practised Larminie's doctrine looked at me as if I'd two heads when I myself at last did read the essay. He told another elder of this strange act, and his friend, to mark the occurrence, enticed John Eglinton, who once knew Larminie, to write a reminiscence of the long-dead pioneer. This was published in *The Dublin Magazine*.

Larminie's essay appeared in *The Contemporary Review*, November 1894, and was called *The development of English Metres*. The part which concerns us is his advocacy of assonance as a metrical device. The idea was a good and a bold one, and merely to have had it and proposed it would have marked out Larminie as a man of exceptional quality. But one is struck as well by the extent of his information and by the signs he gives of having considered very calmly.

He, inevitably, points to the Spanish use of assonance. He explains the gist of the Gaelic system. He cites passages from English verse to show random but impressive employment of assonance, and ends by throwing a slice of the *Iliad* at us to show that the Greeks knew about it.

As an example of his sapience take the underlined sentence in the following extract:

"I must add, however, that in old Irish verse the consonants were by no means neglected. It was recognised that some of them formed more perfect or agreeable concords than others, and for the purpose of guidance there was an elaborate and complete classification made. . . *It would probably be found that something similar would be desirable in employing assonance in English.*"

The final paragraph, in such a survey as ours, is of lively interest:

"It is true that there is a branch of English-writing poets who might be supposed anxious to take the hint. Irish writers would certainly have left their mark upon English literature should they be found to have taken a conspicuous part in the creation of a body of metres having in them the promise of the future, rich with unexhausted possibilities. But it is to be feared that, in spite

of much that might lead one to form an opposite antici-
pation, Irishmen are indisposed to present their ideas to
the world in any but the latest, the most fashionable English garb. Therefore, perhaps, Englishmen, who have more
self-confidence, will make some experiments to encourage
them. Should the experiment fail, my countrymen will
have been spared the trouble of a fruitless effort; in the
event of success, they can then, how much less laboriously,
follow in the beaten track."

I suppose that, in 1894, it was difficult to avoid such
sharp irony; but it is pleasing to think that this essay was
never quite lost sight of; that its prescription is in process
of being compounded, and that, though some Irish poets
are still determinedly eyeing London for the veering of
vogues, yet it is equally possible to show Irish experiments
affecting English poets.

Larminie tried to practise what he preached. In *Fand
and other poems,* a substantial book issued two years before the essay in the *Contemporary,* assonance is frequently used. In *Epilogue* and *Consolation* it alternates
with rhyme:

> If years from winters' chill recover,
> If fields are green and rivers run;
> If thou and I behold each other,
> Hangs it not all on yonder sun?
>
> So while that mighty Lord is gracious
> With prodigal beam to flood the skies,
> Let us be glad that he can spare us
> The light to kindle lovers' eyes.

In some of the lyrics in *Moytura* assonance alone is used:

> Earth has powers benignant;
> They the deadly leading,
> Force their strength unwilling
> Into paths of healing.

Larminie strikes me as that sort of poet who needed to live long in order to achieve fine poetry. He died at forty-nine, and did not, on the whole, succeed in being memorable, except to other Irish poets. Writers with smaller gifts have done more in equal lives, precisely because their gifts were smaller. Larminie was an experimenter, a poet disinclined to be content with well-tried forms, or with the repetition of few forms. Variety and elaboration of structure, as well as novelty and diversity of material, compelled him; and success for such a poet is always deferred. It was not, for example, sufficient for him that he should use assonance, and mix assonance with rhyme, in *abab* quatrains. He used these novelties in diverse schemes of correspondence, and slid and sprang from one modulation to another for the episodes of longer poems.

> Art thou not sad, O sea,
> That o'er thee rest the cloud-banks of the night
> Shot through by no moon-beams?—
> That vainly foam thy waves?
> The darkness knows not they are crested white:
> The darkness heeds not and against its might,
> Striveth thy heart in vain?

The Course of Irish Verse

The lines end: ABACBBC; A and C are assonances, B is rhyme; and there are two lengths of line, running partly with and partly against the correspondences of the line-endings.

His thematic originality is shown by *Fand, Moytura* and *London*. From difficult Gaelic mythology to metropolitan street-scenes was a singular imaginative leap in a single book. Remember the Irish Literary Renaissance was hardly begun, and on the other hand that Henley was only writing his *London Voluntaries* in those same years.

A note upon Douglas Hyde may fittingly follow these notes on William Larminie; the similarity of their interests and aims is sufficiently clear. Hyde was, of course, far less an original poet than Larminie, but gifts of different kinds he had to excess. The one which concerns us here is the gift for translation; if this book were of ampler build, then Douglas Hyde would occupy some very large rooms in it. I have however written at such length about him in my study of the Gaelic translators that I need not dilate upon him here. His influence on the original poets must, however, be remarked.

His palmary achievement, so far as concerns our writing, was the unlocking of the coffers of our oral tradition. He did much in the scholarly way, chronicling, editing and translating older verse and prose; but these things others did besides, in varying degrees and with varying success; while Hyde was the first to make a triumph of the effort to pour abroad the Gaeltacht's cornucopia. He was a collector of genius, and in his *Love-Songs of Connacht, Religious Songs of Connacht, Saints and Sinners* and several other volumes, gathered at last into print some of the finest folk-lore and orally-preserved "art" poetry that has ever been preserved by such means. But of course he was more than a collector; he translated his finds, verse for verse as a rule and prose for prose; and in these translations at their worst there is exciting matter. At their best there is enduring endowment of our literature in English.

These translations did for English-writing poets two things. They revealed to them the splendid excitement of Gaelic song and story, more especially that of the lyric of the Connacht peasant; and they showed them the first large-scale experiment in using the English of the Irish countryman for literary tasks. Those who have read at all in the books of the Irish Literary Movement—if no more than the Essays of Yeats—will not need to be told what instruction and matter for speculation this work of Hyde gave many of our poets. Yeats himself has handsomely acknowledged his debt; Lady Gregory's whole output was given its direction by Hyde; while Synge derived his linguistic theory ultimately from him, and, putting it into effect, prolonged Hyde's influence. This venerable octogenarian, Douglas Hyde, has had one of the fullest, richest, most satisfying and most fructifying lives of any man in Ireland for a hundred years or more; he lived to become President of that State which was established directly by a physical force movement that he reprehended. It is a measure of what our country owes him that the vindicated physical-force men chose him unanimously as the first citizen of Ireland. He lives still, in honoured retirement, with his life's work still affecting the lives of millions.

If I have to epitomise his influence on poetry in English, I must put it like this: he continued, completed and ratified the doctrine that Gaelic literature and history is a prime source and a prime school for the later poet. Without Hyde's books, Hyde's language movement, Hyde's consuming fervour and sway over masses of men, the lesson of a hundred years of verse translation might not have gone home in the end. He summarized that erudition, that literary talent and that glow, in himself; and hardly one poet of quality in Ireland for fifty years has evaded the effect.

I cannot do much in the way of citation from his work; but any Irish anthology will give many examples. Here, for reference, are titles of some which the student must never neglect: *My grief on the sea; Ringleted Youth of my love; The Wife of the Red-haired Man; Bruadair, Smith and Glynn; The Troubled Friar; Joyce's Repentance;* and *Tomaus O Cahan and the Ghost.*

Just to whet the appetite of the reader who is quite unacquainted with this verse, here is a stanza from each of *Ringleted Youth* and *The Red-haired Man:*

> I thought, O my love! you were so—
> As the moon is, or sun on a fountain,
> And I thought after that you were snow,
> The cold snow on top of the mountain;

And I thought after that, you were more
Like God's lamp shining to find me,
Or the bright star of knowledge before,
And the star of knowledge behind me.

●

'Tis what they say,
    Thy little heel fits in a shoe.
'Tis what they say,
    Thy little mouth kisses well, too.
'Tis what they say,
    Thousand loves that you leave me to rue;
That the tailor went the way
    That the wife of the Red man knew.

XV

AFTER HYDE AND LARMINIE, YEATS: WHO OF ALL IRISH poets since Thomas Moore has had widest fame and influence. Coming to him here in this scrutiny of Irish poetry we see that there lay to his hand a cumulus of hints and examples, most of them given by men already dead or directly to die, but some by men who like him were starting for fame. Poets had already been patriots; they already had written upon Irish themes:—land, legend, myth; country, religion, history: already they had translated Gaelic poetry, echoing some of its distinctive music and seizing some of its intensity; while a man here and there had suffused some stanzas with a moment of Irish atmosphere. What was there left, after these, for a Yeats to do?

The Course of Irish Verse

An immensity, we know. To write with manifest genius and illumination, and with multiform development, for nearly five decades. To gather many scatterings. To resolve with deliberation, in response to a vocational urge, to be first and last and all the time an *Irish* poet; and, being this, to be the leader of a literature.

Yeats had deficiencies. By birth, environment and temperament; by philosophic and religious turn of mind; by intellectual bent and custom, he was disposed rather to halt and to counter than to continue and round-off the work of Ferguson and Mangan. (And of course he did so counter as well as round-off their work.)

Yeats was of middle-class Protestant breed; in himself he was fastidious, aloof, subjective, aristocratic rather than not, in fact arrogant; his youth was largely lived away from Ireland, and his schooling within it was shaky; most of his life he "sat loose" to Christianity, being best described perhaps as a latter-day gnostic—as one, that is, who hungered for the arcana of all the cults and the disciplines; coveting more keenly to be mage than saint; a Simon Magus whose purchase-money was poetry. None of these attributes were such as would make him seek to be, or succeed in being, the leader of the Irish as a poet. To the end of his days he lacked Irish; and this was retrogression, and a special fetter in his lifetime; for he lived when the movement for revival began and bore ample fruits.

He had, of course, to counter his deficiencies, many and powerful advantages: genius, the incomparable advantage for whatsoever task, being first.

Were I asked what was special in his genius I should say two things.

This: that there was in him a power, many times shown, to detect in a realm of knowledge wherein he was himself but a dabbler that precise thought, conclusion, illustration or hypothesis, or whatever else it might be, which held some enrichment for his poetry. "He had" Austin Clarke said once to me, though not in exactly this connection, "the forceps."

And this (I would say secondly): his mind had many sides. As a first example I would remark his adaptability, by which—notwithstanding his *hauteur* and aloofness—it was put in his power to be led in his early years to the common people. As a second example I would demonstrate his power to make friendships of spiritual profit to himself. Balancing this power, and killing what was mere self-seeking, he had fires of imagination, a fountain's play of ideas, and a crystalline artistic honour which, between them, repaid his friends; by their virtue he renewed himself, and in doing so renewed them also.

He read himself, talked himself, thought, imagined and befriended himself out of most of his defects; thereby he did what he planned.

Consider him in terms of people—to take one point. Ferguson died when Yeats was two years old, Larminie when he was nineteen, Allingham when he was twenty-five, de Vere when he was eight-and-twenty; Sigerson and Standish James O Grady were vigorous in Yeats's twenties and thirties, while Hyde was his elder contemporary. He knew and learned from most of them, and besides these George Moore, A.E., York Powell, Lionel Johnson, John O Leary and more. The saturnine Synge broke briefly but sharply across his forties; and one might name them continuously up to his death: Augusta Gregory, Maud Gonne, F. R. Higgins and all the others. They enabled him to learn things—sometimes things they knew, sometimes things they did *not* know, or at least did not know that they knew till he learned them from them.

We might even make out what it was he learned from each: from O Grady the myths, from Gregory and Hyde that there were country tales and that country talk could make poetry, from Synge that a hard, sharp, salty zest is inbred in Irish writing. But more to the point than what he learned is what he did with it all.

For one thing, he tweaked the ear of the world and made it turn towards Ireland, to listen to himself, and in some degree to his company. That day when Robert Louis Stevenson praised *Innisfree* was possibly the day when the "sweet, wild twist of Irish song" first charmed our neighbours. Moore pleased them hugely, but seldom with a native style; Rossetti praised Allingham, and other Englishmen other Irishmen; but little long-term attention followed. Yeats first got such attention, and he gets it still; so decidedly does he get it that attack—sure sign that a writer is mattering—has begun among English critics quite lately.

Yeats wrote of Irish myth and country tale, of our history and of our life as he watched it; and others wrote with him; the upshot of which, among other things, is, that matters such as these are well-known to some cultivated persons whose language is English; while those who read creative literature at all in that language are aware that Irish things have been, and have the force to be, the concern of good writers. He mixed un-Irish things with Irish things? Very well, he mixed them. What creative writer of power has ever done otherwise?

But I quote himself on these affairs:

"I thought one day—I can remember the very day when I thought it—'If somebody could make a style which would not be an English style and yet would be musical and full of colour, many others would catch fire from him, and we would have a really great school of ballad poetry in Ireland.'"

"I had a conviction, which indeed I have still, that one's verses should hold, as in a mirror, the colours of one's own climate and scenery in their right proportion; and when I found my verses too full of the reds and yellows Shelley gathered in Italy, I thought for two days of setting things right, not as I should now by making my rhythms faint and nervous and filling my images with a certain coldness, a certain wintry wildness, but by eating little and sleeping upon a board . . .

The Course of Irish Verse

From that day to this I have been busy among the verses and stories that the people make for themselves."

Essay on 'What is popular poetry?' 1901

"... and now a fountain of legends, and, as I think, a more abundant fountain than any in Europe, is being opened, the fountain of Gaelic legends."

The Celtic element in literature 1897

"I would have our writers and craftsmen of many kinds master this history and these legends, and fix upon their memory the appearance of mountains and rivers and make all visible again in their arts, so that Irishmen, even though they had gone thousands of miles away, would still be in their own country."

"I could not now write of any other country but Ireland, for my style has been shaped by the subjects I have worked on ..."

Ireland and the arts 1901

"When Lionel Johnson and Katharine Tynan ... and I, myself, began to reform Irish poetry ... we sought to make a more subtle rhythm, a more organic form, than that of the older Irish poets who wrote in English, but always to remember certain ardent ideas and high attitudes of mind which were the nation itself, so far as a nation can be summarized in the intellect ...

I ... took from Allingham and Walsh their passion for country spiritism, and from Ferguson his pleasure in heroic legend, and while seeing all in the light of European literature, found my symbols of expression in Ireland. . . Here were unwasted passion and precedents in the popular memory for every needed thought and action . . .

"It was our criticism, I think, that set Clarence Mangan at the head of the Young Ireland poets in the place of Davis, and put Sir Samuel Ferguson, who had died with but little fame as a poet, next in the succession."

Poetry and Tradition 1907

None before him in Ireland, of those who wrote English, pondered and harped upon style as he did; on style which arises "out of a deliberate shaping of all things, and from never being swept away, whatever the emotion, into confusion or dullness," on style "which is but high breeding in words and in argument."

Perhaps it was unlikely that any before him should do so. Perhaps it was the Francophil Nineties, bringing over at last from France the zeal of Flaubert, perhaps it was Pater or George Moore or old John Butler Yeats—or all these men and currents going one way—which made it likely that an Irish poet, professedly and in set terms, should worship style.

"Professedly and in set terms" is a needed qualification. There is no native word for "style" in Irish, but if any one thing lasts out through every aberration, through every deformity or lack in Gaelic poetry, that thing is style. Yet Mangan, the best before Yeats of the English-writing poets, was without it. Style as an unsheddable skin was never Mangan's. Wads of his verse were as bad as Gavan Duffy's and fell as entirely out of the climate of literature into that of journalism. This is true of the best we had had, in English. But Yeats is different. Yeats at his worst, Yeats below his own average or that of his inferiors, is still palpably Yeats: style is the skin of his words. "Sometimes" (to quote himself) "it may be, he is permitted the licence of cap and bell, or even the madman's bunch of straws, but he never forgets or leaves at home the seal and the signature."

I may be allowed, perhaps, to gloss one or two of the *dicta* contained in the above quotations.

"One's verses should hold, as in a mirror, the colours of one's own climate and scenery in the right proportion."

This is not simply a striking principle; it is almost a discovery, so far as verse in English is concerned. One tends to take it figuratively, and no doubt it will bear a figurative interpretation, but Yeats meant it first in the simple meaning of his words. He speaks of Shelley's reds and yellows; and his own poems, as everyone knows, shimmer with greys, pearl-pales, cloud-pales, and wan half-lights. When he names colours they are outward as well as inward colours; for was he not son and brother to painters, and schooled for a time himself to palette and brush?

A moment ago I quoted Austin Clarke. I quote him again on this matter. Poets in English, according to Clarke, did not until the Celtic Twilight cease to see about them the hues and the climate of Italy, that country from which they borrowed so lavishly, starting with Chaucer, continuing with Spenser, Wyatt, Shakespeare, the Elizabethans and Dryden, and finding in Rossetti a poet with a title to full borrowing, a title based upon Italian blood. English poetry, says Clarke in effect,* sings of a rain-drenched, hazy, greyish corner of creation as though suns drenched it and lent it Italianate light; while the movement called The Celtic Twilight washed its verse in the regions' rainfalls, dimmed it with its mists, and made its rhymes weatherwise. For that, he says, it has been dubbed romantic, when properly its realism should have been admired.

Yeats dilates upon the ancient legends, and with truth, for they served him in every way: as stories, as symbols and as wells of allusion. Whatever other arsenals he raided, in Byzantium or India or England or Egypt or Greece, or even in his cavernous, glowing heart, the powders of his charges had in them grains of old legend; and his last brief play brings once more on the man Cuchulainn.

"A more subtle rhythm," he says, "a more organic form". . . Style. . . But style defined; style which had in it inherited things, but things as well superadded by himself—the exquisite senses and the spirit of Yeats; his genius for cadence, euphony, wit, and resinous emotion; his skill in ordering and appointing words; his control and submission to control; his antennae always feeling for

---

* I quote from conversation, and the words are my own.

thought, figure, tale and creative impulse. . . Style which is personal and racial, and each because the other. He was an Irish poet.

Thinking of the doubters I had chosen a sheaf of verses to show his Irishry, but revising my words and my argument I leave them aside. Everyone knows them, and those who want to doubt him would doubt him despite them. I am discussing here the ways in which he was an Irish poet, rather than striving to prove him one; the indignity of proof would exceed that of doubt, with such a one as Yeats.

He was Irish, betimes, in a "rebelly" way. I remember that when in 1941 we in the Abbey Theatre commemorated the second anniversary of his death by staging two of his plays and having some of his poems spoken, a woman who came to the performance, and whose feelings one supposes were strongly engaged by the war, charged us with choosing only his "rebelly" poems. We had not done so consciously; indeed we had chosen from every period of his work, and chosen many poems; yet a number really were "rebelly", among them *Easter 1916,* and *The Ballad of Roger Casement,* the one which jibes at John Bull and declares that

The ghost of Roger Casement is beating on the door.

But of course Yeats was Irish at other times than when he was baiting John Bull, or lighting lamps to Pearse and Casement. He was Irish when he foamed about "the daily

spite of this unmannerly town" or stigmatized some Irishmen as "Paudeen fumbling in the greasy till"; and still
Irish when he made current the unfounded rumour that

> Romantic Ireland's dead and gone:
> It's with O Leary in the grave.

I do not mean simply that this was an angry lover's talk
—though it *was* that, of course: only a lover could be
struck so hurtfully or could smart aloud so wrathfully. But
I mean more than that. I mean that he drew the common,
current wrangles and collisions of Irish affairs deep within
his poetry, and that instead of sinking his poetry he raised
these affairs.

Furthermore the tempest of his scorn was Irish; and
his being so vulnerable to calumnious tongues. If often
there were on the one side the mass of the Irish, and he
himself only or few beside him on the other, then the words
of Thomas MacDonagh to his court-martial judges in
1916 might have helped him:

"We do not claim," MacDonagh said, "to represent
the people of Ireland; we claim to represent the intellect
and the immortal soul of Ireland."

A man may differ from millions of his own, and, in the
very act and moment of differing, show common blood
and ultimate community of cause with them. This was
sometimes Yeats's act. But then too he spoke *for* the Irish,
in the simpler sense. To Pearse he was the man "who in

our time (in *Cathleen Ni Houlihan*) has best given expression to Irish Nationalism"; and apart from opinions he brought the Irishman's *voice*—its inflexions, cadences and idioms—into verse. The wavering, unemphasized rhythms, and the half-hushed, murmuring music, have been most remarked; but MacDonagh judged that even the line of seven syllables came through. In his last years what he most desired to make was a balladry akin to that which Higgins had found in Mayo.

Again one must remember this, that despite his early love for Verlaine's *dictum* about strangling rhetoric, he saw that the Irish loved eloquence, and became the only good Irish poet except Mangan to make eloquent lyrical poetry. His *Red Hanrahan's Song about Ireland* is consummate eloquence in lyric; I surmise that it was made to the verbal tune of Mangan's *Kathaleen Ny Houlihan,* which again was got from O Heffernan, who got it from O Bruadair.

If religious care for finesse in one's craft be Irish—and Gaelic metric suggests it is—then Yeats was Irish. His last poem begins (to the fury of poets in Ireland, and this again is witness): *Irish poets learn your trade.* One of the first he ever wrote begins: *Words alone are certain good.*

If what the world, or anyhow the English world, avers of us is true: that we vary swiftly in mood: then Yeats is Irish. He has tenderness, quietness, pity; rage, love and lust; gaiety, fantasy, indignation; robustness, delicacy, arrogance . . . how many more passions and spiritual weathers? Mockery and reverence surely.

The Course of Irish Verse

Since I am not disputing politics, I do not set down these notions from the motive some might find in them, the motive of silencing those Irish critics who would hand Yeats over to the English, who indeed very frequently speak as though they owned him and who seldom know we have other poets in Ireland. I set them down to show that, after many decades, an abundant and grandly-achieving poet had come who was certainly Irish, and Irish in subtle as well as in evident ways, "shaking his scourges" over us, as well as tilling our fields.

One matter more I must speak of: the theatre which Yeats and others gave us. They were like surgeons who, by making a tiny correction in the action of a gland, free the body for some necessary and hitherto-impeded function. That the Irish made no Gaelic drama suggests an aberrant gland in the race; for they strike all observers, and themselves equally, as made for drama. They sense and relish it hourly, they are dramatic in speech and often in act. Yet they hardly can be said to have given a playwright to the world before the eighteenth century. In that century the Dublin theatres were busy, but the playwrights we remember best wrote not for them but for England. In the nineteenth century the fact was unchanged; hence Goldsmith, Sheridan, Congreve, Wilde and Shaw are more England's than ours. England needed them almost as badly as we; but this was small comfort to us.

But then at the start of the present century Yeats, A. E., George Moore, Hyde, Lady Gregory, the Fays and others provided the beginnings of an Irish drama. It was in part universal as well; but the Universe needed less to rejoice than we: we had nothing of our own before.

One after another the arts were entering our ambit. There was science before, scholarship in letters and history; and then came the art of translation. There were scholars of folk-music, Bunting and others; and original poets followed, translating first and afterwards repeating the designs of the poems they brought over, composing poems to the tunes the Buntings saved, and transferring the verbal tunes to poems not made for music. Statuary followed some way; at least such a sculptor as Hogan made living stone of Davis and Daniel O Connell. Novelists attempted to get into the swim, though not for some decades did they catch the stroke. And now in the first of the nineteen-hundreds the mesmeric, popular art of the theatre fell into line. . . As we know, painting, with a story like that of the Irish theatre, followed; and stained-glass-making; and finally story-telling found its stroke and swam. . . And into the theatre flowed all the comminglings which Ireland was and was grasping to be.

Poetry got into that theatre, because Yeats was in it; and genius in acting got in because the Fays joined him.

The English theatre just then was empty of poetry; it was empty of everything, to speak quite justly: people talked nothings on the stage and people heard nothings on their benches. Shakespeare survived, as a "vehicle" for actor-managers; but that was all, till Shaw, Granville-

Barker and some more set to. That is why this Irish literary theatre made Ireland important at the time.

Irish letters, with Yeats, became a movement. Not that he was a demi-urge setting everyone else on the move. Hyde, for instance, had his own electric turbines, and was pressing-down the switches in many a house in Ireland. Neither do I mean to credit Yeats with all the attributes and plaudits of a leader; there are signs he was divided between the wish to lead, and the wish to leave behind, other writers. What I do mean is this: that, partly willy and partly nilly, Yeats gave cohesion; around about him writers had a common aim, and though often at issue as persons they were generally grouped as artists.

No one reason will ever explain a human fact, and a full explanation of this relative community would take us far. But Yeats was one prime cause of it. First because his keel was sharp, and cut such a trough in our literary sea that the waves around flowed into it. Second because among his endowments was that of discerning and stating aims; for all his talk of dreams he was the broad-awake kind of artist, the Ronsard, the Ibsen, the Wagner, the Eliot, the one who is interiorly compelled not only to innovate but beyond innovation to say what it is he innovates; to find and to promulgate the luminous and fructifying formulae. This sort of artist needs others; his work must be buttressed, spread and prolonged. Therefore he unified our letters and made a movement.

XVI

WE KNOW THE MEN AND WOMEN WHO MADE THE MOVE-
ment with him, and the names which follow after theirs.
Among the first class A. E. (George Russell) has a special
place.

He knew Yeats when both were youths, and admired
and lauded him for forty years, while for most of that time
in addition he supplied to younger men that kindly, generous, personal aid (so essential in a movement) which
Yeats was by temperament hardly fitted to give so continuously and copiously. All remember that about A. E. . . .
Doubtless his art was less than that of Yeats; but he had
his individual facets, and diversified the total achievement. If we think of Yeats as, in some way, the fertile but
careless father of some of these writers, then A. E. may
be called the careful midwife who delivered them alive,
and the wet-nurse who suckled them to strength. He even
had by him the sheets on which to lay them: the sheets of
his *Irish Statesman,* which he edited for years.

Distinct and rich personality is affluence, in any kind of
work whatsoever, but more in the arts than in most; and
this red-faced, bulky, bespectacled, hairy Armagh-man, an
assemblage of shrewdness, mysticism, poetry, and eco-
nomic and political inquisitiveness, was a godsend. He
tended in ways to deflect the prevailing winds of the Irish
tradition; but winds are not easy to change, and we need
not be fearful; the signs are we shall choose and reject

from what he offered, according to its healthfulness or noxiousness.

Thus A. E.'s pantheistic Earth-worship on the one hand, and on the other the voracity for land of the Irish peasant, are both comprehensible phenomena in Ireland, being each a deformation of the passionate and reverent regard of the Christian as he looks on the "proliferating mould", the creature and the limited manifestation of a God transcendent yet immanent.

Thus again in A. E.'s words and work, through the whole of his life, the spirit's primacy meant much more than art. He was ascetic, devout and charitable, and insistent upon the fact and the value of mystical experience; hence a predominantly Catholic people may honour him and gain by his example, shedding his exotic and erroneous tenets, and remembering as part of the greater wisdom of their teachers a cardinal truth A. E. did not know: that mystical experience is pure gift of God, and not to be induced at will by drill for the spirit. Thus corrected, his life is a noble witness. The religious sense abides in Irish poetry, and A. E. is Irish in possessing it.

Un-Irish indeed he was in suffering through his spiritual perception a dimming of the sensuous world. Few wrote poetry less earthy than he, the Earth-worshipper; for among the major wants of his verse is want of sensuousness. His poems are never tactile; the ear finds them thin, on the whole; and even the eye, though A. E. was a painter, finds lack of particularity and of variousness of colour. Besides he is hardly concerned in his verse with the hues of human character, or, save in *The Dark Lady,* which is a "sport" in his work, with the chameleon passions of men.

In all these lacks, which are really one, he was un-Irish. Add to them this, to conclude our catalogue, that A. E. the poet was incurious in matters of craft; his technical armature was simple, the same, you might say, at the end as it was at the start. He was no experimenter.

It remains true that his verse has Irish lineaments, other than spirituality and mystical glow. At perhaps his nearest approach to particularity he seconds Yeats in picturing our skies and weathers: and then his lines shimmer, dissolve and slide like our secret half-lights and our brief, multiple minglings of sun and vapour and rain. He absorbed our mythology and employed, insubstantially, suggestions from our fairy lore; and he played those slurring spinet-rhythms begun by Callanan in English.

A. E. lost more than Yeats through ignorance of Irish: it might have humanised his too rarefied verse, and mixed in humour or the rich by-products of humour with it; it might too have made his tunes more plangent when they needed be; perhaps sharpened also his blunted dramatic sense. Some say his use of mythology was poor, because he knew the myths at second hand; but this seems to me illegitimate criticism. A poet is not bound to take any material as he finds it, nor is he less Irish for passing old tales through his personal spectrum. Whether one prefers the older or newer versions is quite beside the point.

The Course of Irish Verse

We remark in these two, in Yeats and A. E., an additional talent, one not to be found before them in an Irish writer, unless we count Davis as such. I mean the talent of the bellman, the billposter, the advertising agent; and do not mistake me, I count this addition among the gains of Irish letters: every Irish writer, if no other Irishman, is keenly aware how distinctly its absence can confine the effect of their art.

It was not just Yeats's genius as a poet which threw new shadows on the screens of the world, but his way of persuading the world that they must be thrown. He was fortunate in looking like a poet: they tell us few poets do: he was lucky in talking like a poet—not all of them do; moreover, through his father, he had enviable friendships with most of those who dictated the arts in England. But it may be that these were secondary helps, and he just had a genius for gospelling. Gospel he did to advantage anyhow: through him the Americans and English attended to our writing as never before or since. If Shaw played *Cornet-di-Bassetto,* Yeats played the trumpet, an instrument a little more refined but sounding as far.

A. E.'s propaganda was simpler, and even more unselfish. He displayed an improbable capacity for journalism, for writing, that is, upon current subjects in a manner at once rapid, varied and quickly-understood. His writing in this mode had, as journalism has, the object of instant effect; but of course he evaded the journalist's penalty, slapdashness. For years his subsidised weekly, *The Irish Statesman,* dinned into readers the excellence of Irish writing; its bankruptcy was a disaster, and its place has not been taken.

Because A. E. is only ten years dead, and because most of his poems which look like lasting have all for decades been current in anthologies, those which are quotable here will be very familiar. I will quote very few for that reason.

The wavering rhythm and religious mood are in *Immortality*:

> We must pass like smoke or live within the spirit's fire;
> For we can no more than smoke unto the flame return
> If our thought has changed to dream, our will unto desire,
> As smoke we vanish though the fire may burn.

And in *Remembrance*:

> There were many burning hours on the heartsweet tide,
> And we passed away from ourselves, forgetting all
> The immortal moods that faded, the god who died,
> Hastening away to the King on a distant call.

In *Carrowmore* the sing-song of an older English metre is made to carry the interpenetration of the visible world and the Land of Youth, in a typical Celtic Twilight poem:

> It's a lonely road through bogland to the lake at Carrow-
> more,
> And a sleeper there lies dreaming where the water laps the
> shore;
> Though the moth-wings of the twilight in their purples are
> unfurled,
> Yet his sleep is filled with music by the masters of the world.

There's a hand is white as silver that is fondling with his
   hair:
There are glimmering feet of sunshine that are dancing by
   him there:
And half-open lips of faery that were dyed a faery red
In their revels where the Hazel Tree its holy clusters shed.

Oh, the great gates of the mountain have opened once
   again,
And the sound of song and dancing, falls upon the ears of
   men,
And the Land of Youth lies gleaming, quick with rainbow
   light and mirth,
And the old enchantment lingers in the honey-heart of
   earth.

Typical also is *A Call of the Sidhe,* where the rhythm
combines with the other factors, and where A. E. signs his
fairies more certainly with his own mark, seeing them, not
as casual, disconnected "sports" of the spiritual world, but
as one more kind of elementals:

Drink: the immortal waters quench the spirit's longing.
Art thou not, bright one, all sorrow past, in elation,
Made young with joy, grown brother-hearted with the
   vast,
Whither thy spirit wending flits the dim stars past
Unto the Light of Lights in burning adoration.

A. E. did not work with Yeats's thoroughness on all that
made up his poems. He is capable, in his third book,

of inversions which Yeats rejected soon after *Inisfree,* and of a well-rubbed diction ("in elation"); there are hints as well that he shared some phrases with the better poet. Better poets sometimes appropriate casts of phrasing from poets less good, so we cannot say for certain who first made images like "moth-wings of the twilight" or thought of the fairies as dancers; but Yeats seems generally to have had them earlier in print.

But A. E., I say it again, has his personal accent. It is in *Reconciliation*:

> I begin through the grass once again to be bound to the Lord;
> I can see, through a face that has faded, the face full of rest
> Of the earth, of the mother, my heart with her heart in accord,
> As I lie mid the cool, green tresses that mantle her breast
> I begin with the grass once again to be bound to the Lord.

And it is, somehow, notwithstanding the English cast of the diction, in his sonnet on Terence MacSwiney; for a soul's force to downface its enemies, among them the clamours of its own protesting flesh, was something A. E. with the whole of his being revered. He was transported by this incontestable demonstration that

> There is that within us can conquer the dragon pain,
> And go to death alone, slowly and unafraid.

Spirit responded to spirit, and the dying hunger-striker and the gladdened poet gave double expression to the Irishman's passion for spiritual gold.

XVII

SPIRITUAL GOLD WAS THE ONE KIND A. E. EVER HAD, AND once when he wished to publish a collection of poems by a group of new poets he went to Lord Dunsany for the money to pay for it. "Dunsany", said Yeats, "I hear you're providing groundsel for A. E.'s canaries."

The laugh was with Dunsany, for some of those canaries have justified the poet-bird-fancier by singing very sweetly on their groundsel. They included Pádraic Colum, Seumas O Sullivan, and Thomas MacDonagh.

XVIII

O SULLIVAN, OF ALL WHO WERE YOUNGER THAN YEATS and A. E., wrote the most like them, more like A. E. than like Yeats, however. The same fluttering rhythms; the poems about fairies—written with a possibly more delicate melody than A. E.'s, and less earthy passion than Yeats's; the same limning of fleeting lights and vanishing movements; the same gravity of temper, which was less heavy heart than savouring mind.

There are, of course, differences: the vignettes of city life, slight as they are, denote the Dubliner; there is a

quiet interest in the gentler beasts which neither of the
elders showed; there is a Nationalist feeling which began
before Insurrection or hunger-strike; and other personal
tints there are too: the more urbane, more worldly wit,
for instance.

> It is a whisper among the hazel bushes;
> It is a long low whispering voice that fills
> With a sad music the bending and swaying rushes;
> It is a heart-beat deep in the quiet hills.

> Twilight people, why will you still be crying,
> Crying and calling to me out of the trees?
> For under the quiet grass the wise are lying,
> And all the strong ones are gone over the seas.

That movement is Gaelic, though the image it fetches
up is the quick, almost-stepless walk of the Oriental; and
the iteration of vowels—*Twilight, crying, crying, quiet,
wise, lying; strong, gone*—Gaelic too. The mysteriousness
also comes out of the hazes of Ireland; but I have a faint
doubt about the scented sadness: *that* is the perfume from
Pre-Raphaelite womankind. And from where, if not from
the haze-muted coasts and moorlands, came the cobweb
lightness of *The Sheep* and *The Poplars,* the withdrawn
and musing slowness of *The Herdsman?* They differ in
their way of haunting from the English, and even from the
Scottish, ways. Compare them with *Goblin Market, La
Belle Dame Sans Merci, The Witch's Ballad,* and *Nymp-
hidia.*

87

The Course of Irish Verse

As I went dreaming
By the grey poplar trees,
They bent down and whispered
Words like these:

"In a far country
Is a lonely glen,
Hushed with the footfall
Of shadowy men.

Shadowy and silent,
And grey amongst the trees
That have long fotgotten
The sound of the breeze."

●

O herdsman driving your slow twilight flock
By darkening meadow and hedge and grassy rath;
The trees stand shuddering as you pass by;
The suddenly falling silence is your path.

The nearest verse we had had to this was Ferguson's *The Fairy Thorn;* and surely O Sullivan's fairies are more immaterial, more like momentary tremblings of air, than even Yeats's?

From our hidden places
By a secret rath,
We troop in the moonlight
To the edge of the green rath.

There the night through
We take our pleasure,
Dancing to such a measure
As earth never knew,

To song and dance
And lilt without a name,
So sweetly breathed
Twould put a bird to shame.

•

Music so forest wild
And piercing sweet, would bring
Silence on blackbirds singing
Their best in the ear of spring.

•

Oh many a thrush and blackbird
Would fall to the dewy ground
And pine away in silence
For envy of such a sound.

The Dublin we discover in Yeats is a city of opinions—
a city, we may phrase it afresh, of contending lives. In
Stephens, again, the city emerges and vanishes, a starting-
place for personal caprice, for just one poet's play. It is,
in O Sullivan, the actual, palpable Dublin: a town with
named streets wherein everyday doings are astir. *In Mer-
cer Street, Nelson Street, The Piper, The Funeral, The
Ragman, The Lamp-lighter* and *In Merrion Square*—
these have the distinction of reminding our poets and their
readers that Ireland includes some cities, and, specifically,
that Dublin is an ancient portion of Ireland. The reminder
extends our matter; while its conveyance in verse is a
genuine extension of our craft. These are not master-
poems; but they *are* successful and truly individual; and

they have in their lines, for all their modest appearance, an original view which does constitute an advance.

One detects in O Sullivan that feeling for religion which is seldom indeed far off from the Irish pen. It shows in him, be it said, in a curious way: sometimes with plain Christianity; sometimes with a semi-"literary" lamenting for a mythical Golden Age of Paganism; sometimes with a fleeting, undecided grimace at a particular creed. It runs behind, rather than through, the lines, but is certainly there.

XIX

EVEN WHEN GOOD POETS RESEMBLE ONE ANOTHER, HOW distinct they remain. O Sullivan, for example, resembles, yet is clearly marked-off from, Yeats and A. E.; and likewise Joseph Campbell is no one but himself. He could not have merged in the shadow or the light of any other; for he had not alone a different gift but a different storehouse.

In that storehouse, I hinted already, no writer before him had even done stocktaking, let alone lightened the shelves; in it, since Gaelic bardry ceased, the store was unstirred—the store of the life of the North-East corner of Ireland.

Ferguson glimpsed and at once went blind to it—anyhow to all that was specially its own.

Cecil Alexander touched it and held it; then allowed it to fall.

A. E. walked out of it to Dublin, bringing nothing of it with him for his poetry.

Then Joseph Campbell left; but his bag was packed for the road.

For, although Joseph Campbell made Wicklow his cenobite's cell, where he lived before and after living in America, Antrim the whole time had a strong living hand in his verse. In Wicklow he died, alone, at night, his head on his hearth; but his head as he laid it down, I'll swear, was not quite emptied of Antrim. I had heard him reminisce aloud a while before of an aunt who, when he was a child, would say to some of them: "Come gather around me, childher, till I count our kindred." That was the sort of store Joseph Campbell kept.

For years I was unsure of the source of the folk-lore I found in *The Mountainy Singer;* but suddenly I saw that its tang had been brought from Scotland. For the point about this North-East Ireland is its nearness to the other Scot-land. Campbell was a simple man, with both kinds of simplicity: the kind which over-simplifies, and the kind which never complicates. So simple was he that he saw what was under his nose: the semi-Scottish English spoken around him; the tatters of Gaelic; and the mingling—or at least the jumbling-together—of Gaelic legend and Scottish country tale. Even the Catholic legends had a special savour; and these things went to his verse.

He was a pure poet. I grasped this fact more surely than before when last I re-read *The Mountainy Singer*. Here was *immediacy*:—that seemingly-natural chording of poetry's notes (its sense, sound, images and motion) which makes a poem appear as if born entire, and not made piecemeal. Things born may have blemishes, but they all are *beings;* and a poem with the air of a being just cannot be faked, by even the cleverest, by even the most tireless talent. Genius wombs it.

Let me credit Campbell with genius, and I'll grant you genius leans on talent and is awkward without it, and that Campbell's talent was small. Does this explain why years of his life were intractable to poetry? Twelve years in the States, and how few good lines he bought with them, he who had called himself Pedlar. He had better stock going than returning, and had published the bulk of his best-made poems by his middle thirties. He lacked the stamina of talent, but possessed the initial creativeness of genius, and the poems his genius made can move us and delight us. They include much song of the simplest sort, carefree things one sings without company, and things which are deeply emotional; the unforged signature of song is on them all.

The Ulster musicians, Hamilton Harty and Herbert Hughes, gloved them with music, and made good hands of them; hundreds sing them who never heard Campbell's name, and I myself knew *The Ninepenny Fidil* before I knew poems were made, instead of happening like grass.

Campbell's simplicity reached to the nursery rhyme. Imagine a child whose earliest speech was poetry, and *My mother has a wee red shoe* might easily be what it

said. Any child would get it by rote for pleasure. . . But
the simple man is a sage, and the sage in Campbell spoke
oracular words—as always, about root things: about
death and birth and love and soil, and crop and stone and
water; and the Root of all roots: God. He would say
naively, "William Blake has influenced me." His successful oracularities saved his claim from being mocked: one
could fancy Blake being able to bear such lines as these:

> The silence of unlaboured fields
> Lies like a judgment on the air.

He had another influence: Gaelic poetry. He had Irish
enough to teach a class in New York; he talked the language with relish as far as it took him; and his character
had atavistic kinship with Meyer's Nature poets. This too
he claimed, but did not need to claim: it was patent; his
living a little like Marbhán and Cellach, in a "shieling"
among oaktrees, was more than Romanticism. He had
something of their ways of writing, with clean, sharp pen,
eyes of primeval keenness, and mind turned outward. He
had the Irish racial absorption in character of high relief;
we have it as an instinct, but in him it was confirmed and
turned one way by Synge, whose cult of shuiler, tinker and
the clan of wind and ditch made Irish letters and art for
a while Borrovian. So we get from Campbell *The Dwarf*
and *The Tinker,* and finally, in *Irishry,* a poetic portfolio
of drawings of Irish Types.

He was eminently fitted to portray these types, if acquaintance for fifty years and pleasure in their company sufficed. Even in his closing years in Lackendarragh his chosen company assembled in an old-time cottage, where an elderly, illiterate glensman, to quote his own highly quotable account of it, "had started the second row around the fire." I recall Joseph Campbell tramping the downhill road from Glencree to Enniskerry, contentedly talking to (I think) a country blacksmith, and telling of his pleasure in the quaint craft-words of such men. He respected himself and them too much to sentimentalise them; and even in intimacy insisted on his quality of poet, for which they must mark him. Many of them did.

All things in Campbell may be summed in one, that his taproot dug to the deeps of the Irish ground, while his ·rootlets raked it for nutriment.

As a sign there was his relish for the Gaelic thing, just now remarked, which never felt staleness or sourness; *his* being that kind of talismanic spirit in which lived the young leaves' greenness, the morning purity, the April heavens of the start of the revival. The disillusionments and dusts of much subsequent history left its lustres untouched for him; and his vivid, retentive memory preserved it stainless.

Folklore charmed him: his mind was made for its study and was steeped and dyed in it; in talk he retailed it and theorised around it. He believed, like A. E., in the poet as seer; and his eye, like A. E.'s, expanded the visible world. Beyond A. E., however, Campbell devoured the "solid-seeming" world; Ireland especially; Wicklow and Antrim over all. Unlike Yeats he could never crow and toss his comb

> Because God-appointed Berkeley had proved all things a
> dream;

nor could he think of what he looked-on, touched with pleasure, tasted, smelt and listened-to, as

> This pragmatical, preposterous pig of a world.

He withdrew, indeed, from cities; but animal and plant and bird, and cloud and river and old stones "compelled his imagination many days."

His name is all but unknown in England, and of that he neither would have nor should have complained: for, excepting for Johnson, Blake and a few more artists, England, for Campbell, might not have been there at all. It might have been chauvinism: it really was detachment.

His books, which are not very many, have been long out of print; it will not, on that account, be wrong to quote four or five of his poems. The first I mentioned was *The Ninepenny Fidil;* here is some of it:

> My father and mother were Irish,
> And I am Irish too;
> I bought a wee fidil for ninepence,
> And it is Irish too.
> I'm up in the morning early
> To greet the dawn of day,

And to the lintwhite's piping
The many's the tune I play.

One pleasant eve in June-time
I met a lochrie-man:
His hands and feet were weazen,
His height was not a span.
He boo'r'd me for my fidil—
"You know," says he, "like you,
My father and mother were Irish,
And I am Irish too!"

He took my wee red fidil,
And such a tune he turned—
The Glaise in it whispered,
The Lionan in it m'urned.
Says he "My lad, you're lucky—
I wish t' I was like you:
You're lucky in your birth-star,
And in your fidil too!"

Roger Quilter set to music one of his songs in which the
word-music is fine:

I will go with my father a-ploughing
To the green fields by the sea,
And the rooks and the crows and the sea-gulls
Will come flocking after me.
I will sing to the patient horses
With the lark in the white of the air,
And my father will sing the plough-song
That blesses the cleaving-share.

96

The Gilly of Christ is one of his famous things, and has
that Scottish tinge I spoke of:

> I am the gilly of Christ,
> The mate of Mary's Son;
> I run the roads at seeding-time,
> And when the harvest's done.
>
> I sleep among the hills,
> The heather is my bed;
> I dip the termon-well for drink,
> And pull the sloe for bread.
>
> No eye has ever seen me,
> But shepherds hear me pass,
> Singing at fall of even
> Along the shadowed grass.
>
> The beetle is my bellman,
> The meadow-fire my guide,
> The bee and bat my ambling-nags
> When I have need to ride.
>
> All know me only the Stranger,
> Who sits on the Saxon's height;
> He burned the bacach's little house
> On last Saint Brigid's night.
>
> He sups off silver dishes,
> And drinks in a golden horn,
> But he will wake a wiser man
> Upon the Judgment Morn!

I am the Gilly of Christ,
The mate of Mary's Son;
I run the roads at seeding-time
And when the harvest's done.

The seed I sow is lucky,
The corn I reap is red,
And whoso sings the Gill's Rann
Will never cry for bread.

Since I spoke of his use of "that semi-Scottish dialect"
here is an instance:

'Tis pretty tae be in Baile-liosan,
Tis pretty tae be in green Magh-Luan;
Tis pretty tae be in Newtownbreda,
Beeking under the eaves of June.
The cummers are out wi' their knitting and spinning.
The thrush sings frae his crib on the wa',
And o'er the white road the clachan caddies
Play at their marlies and goaling-ba'.

You see: he sings.

XX

FROM NORTHERNER TO MIDLANDMAN, FROM CAMPBELL
TO Pádraic Colum.

Concerning Colum the writer one does not ask, Is he
Irish? The query rather is, What is not Irish in him? He

is of Catholic country family, with a mind like—what shall I say?—like one of those firkins of butter they find in bogs. None know what year long since they were laid in cool, wet places, and not remembered; only that it *was* long since and that still to-day they are here, are still as fresh as this morning's churning, and carry from an age that used be, in a land still here, the sweetness of grass once chewed to the milk that made them. Such is Colum's mind: an ancient mind full of newness.

He was born of the native Irish, but, by learning our language, country-lore, mythology and history, increased his nativeness. It would even seem, as one reads him, that these things in turn grew more Irish passing through his mind. That is, I know, a singularly odd thing to say; but one needs an odd way of putting things to suggest the nativeness of Colum. His novel *Castle Conquer,* his Abbey Theatre plays, his travel volumes and his poetry, all have the ageless, ample midland placidity: graciousness, mildness, and cautious, deliberate living, compounded with reverie and the quieter sorts of song: though a rill of the hot Connacht blood from across the border would seem to have got into him, preserving him from Midland flatness. His most evident weakness is the same as Allingham's; an inability to sustain long works. This makes his novel episodic, and *The Story of Lowry Maen*, his epic on the coming of the Iron Age to Ireland, prosy.

I have heard of poets in England who could see very little in Colum, and who wondered politely at our constant praise of him. They may be right; he may have little for them; but I never heard an Irishman decry him. We yield to his work as to something in the Irish grain—our climate's kind of light, the prevailing direction of our winds, our own sorts of stone and soil. His feeling for high moods in politics might strike an outsider as at issue with the quiet of his mind, but for us it is additional proof that he is Irish; for, quiet mind or brawling mind, the Irishman follows the public action with interest. The sonnet on Arthur Griffith was predictable, as was, in another way, the way of that extraregional rill of hotter blood, the ballad on the death of Roger Casement. Did we forget that blood the anguish and the violence of hatred in the ballad might startle us:

> They have hanged Roger Casement to the tolling of a bell,
> *Ochone, och, ochone, ochone!*
> And their Smiths, and their Murrays, and their Cecils say
>   it's well,
> *Ochone, och, ochone, ochone!*
> But there are outcast peoples to lift that spirit high,
> Flayed men and breastless women who labour fearfully,
> And they will lift him, lift him, for the eyes of God to see,
> And it's well, after all, Roger Casement.

That spirit of agony and rage recalls Davis' *Lament for Owen Roe.*

The Old Woman of the Roads, The Drover, Cradle Song and *The Terrible Robber Men* are classics of the movement; countless anthologies and hordes of singers have made of them household words.

O I wish the sun was bright in the sky,
And the fox was back in his den, O!
For always I'm hearing the passing-by
Of the terrible robber men, O!
The terrible robber men.

O! what does the fox carry over the rye
When it's bright in the morn again, O!
And what is it making the lonesome cry
With the terrible robber men, O!
The terrible robber men.

Here is the genuine folk-song:

I went out in the evening, my sweetheart for to find;
I stood by her cottage window, as well I do mind;
I stood by her cottage window, and I thought I would get in,
But instead of pleasures for me my sorrows did begin!

Fine colour had my darling though it was not me was there:
I did not sit beside her, but inside there was a pair!
I stood outside the window like a poor neglected soul,
And I waited till my own name was drawn across the coal.

Colum is one of the poets who has worthily translated Gaelic poetry; and one of these translations which is well-known to his readers is *The Poor Girl's Meditation,* a rendering of one of the *Love-Songs of Connacht.* It illustrates the almost indolent facility with which this poet succeeds. I look from Hyde's literal version to the original Irish, and back to Colum, and I say: Here's Colum doing it again, finding the easy thing, the poem that wants only the tip of a finger to throw it into perfect shape. You have that sensation with many of his poems; you see him taking a flawed ballad and righting it, or borrowing a setting and a refrain —as in his *Girls Spinning*—and fitting a few simple but faultless country songs into the setting, to make very pleasing poetry of all. (The last citation above is from *Girls Spinning*.) You have the sensation that everything he gives has rolled down the hill to him; whereas other poets have to climb the hill for everything. Colum seems only a third of the time to originate—and perhaps that is why so many of his poems are so *right,* why many find him the most Irish of living poets: he is always seeing and hearing what is the very stuff of Ireland, and just giving it an added graciousness, a colouring, a less hoarse tune of words, a correction of phrasing. In all probability this is only the deceptiveness of considerable art, which does its work so entirely as to seem to have done no work.

Here is *The Poor Girl's Meditation*:

> I am sitting here,
> Since the moon rose in the night;
> Kindling a fire,
> And striving to keep it alight:
> The folk of the house are lying
> In slumber deep;
> The cocks will be crowing soon:
> The whole of the land is asleep.
>
> May I never leave this world
> Until my ill-luck is gone;
> Till I have cows and sheep,

And the lad that I love for my own:
I would not think it long,
The night I would lie at his breast,
And the daughters of spite, after that,
Might say the thing they liked best.

Love covers up hate,
If a girl have beauty at all:
On a bed that was narrow and high,
A three-month I lie by the wall:
When I bethought on the lad
That I left on the brow of the hill,
I wept from dark until dark,
And my cheeks have the tear-tracks still.

And, O, young lad that I love,
I am no mark for your scorn:
All you can say of me
Is undowered I was born:
And if I've no fortune in hand,
Nor cattle nor sheep of my own,
This I can say, O lad,
I am fitted to lie my lone.

Colum's verse, like Campbell's, is a house full of people, with fields and roads around it which are filled with people as well. He does not so often make his own thoughts into poems, preferring to project inside them the women and men he knows and moves among. This is a way of saying that he cultivates the dramatic lyric, which has been for many hundreds of years an indigenous form in Ireland. He is a finer dramatist than Campbell, and fitted of right into the company of the early Abbey Theatre; and the bent for drama shows in his poems; they are not only dramatic lyrics, but often have a dramatic framework, being written in sets, where each reacts on the others.

Many a poet is compelled by his own nature to brood on that of his fellow-man; but not every such poet broods affectionately. Colum's style is warm, human, friendly; and the friendliness shows in many of his subjects and comments. He wrote with love of Casement, Griffith, Kuno Meyer and other notable people; but, besides these, of the unnoted country folk of his youth.

Our chief grumble against Pádraic Colum is that he gives one a taste for a wine which he draws in too small a quantity. Whether it is his long-drawn exile, or some other cause, his poems have been so far too few in number. A dozen books like *Wild Earth* would have been a cellar for a lifetime.

XXI

PADRAIC COLUM'S NAME AND JAMES STEPHENS'S NAME go often together in talk about Irish poetry; but rather because they are distinguished coevals than because of a sharp resemblance in their work. There is in fact at least as much difference as resemblance. Colum's first book was entitled *Wild Earth;* Stephens's *Insurrections...*

Had Synge not spoken a short while before him, this first book by Stephens, published in May in 1909, must have startled the Irish poets and their readers halfway out of their wits. Forewarned as they were, and thus in part forearmed, the insurrections must still have struck them as out of all measure crude; the "yawp" as barbaric beyond the needs of new poets. Synge himself, besides, for all his Lawrencian plea that poetry turn to brutality again to find new force, even Synge in his plays, the main things he wrote, had clad his brute in the fig-leaves of humour and in the daisy-chains of country images. One might, without fetching things too far, make him, John Millington Synge, a begetter of transatlantic "toughness" in writing; of himself it is still to be noted that his clay-and-worm-y words occur chiefly in his poetry; and these were not gathered in a book until five months after *Insurrections*. So Stephens's poems were well named.

I remember the first of the talkie films to come to Ireland, and the year it came: *The Singing Fool,* 1929. I remember the soundless awe in which we first heard words from a screen—yes, indeed, and how raucous the vaudeville voices of America seemed to our ears. We had not grown up with those voices . . . To those who grew up with Stephens's elders in poetry he must have seemed as raucous as did Al Jolson to us. To see that it was poetry must have taken those readers some time. I lament that I was only one age with the book; I should love to have heard—as heard I vow I should have—the fluent abuse surround it; abuse like that which now surrounds the writings of the thirties and forties. Within three years there were two reprintings, but these prove little: shocks often pay. Here is a part of the opening poem:

The Course of Irish Verse

I will not dance:
I say I will not dance.
Your audience, pah, let them go home again,
Sleek, ugly pigs. Am I to hop and prance
As long as they will pay,
And posture for their eyes, and lay
My womanhood before them? Let them drain
Their porter-pots and snuffle—I'll not stay . . .

This was not a Trembling, but a Rending, of the Veil. This, succeeding to *The Wind Among the Reeds, The Earth-Breath, The Love-Songs of Connacht, The Mountainy Singer* and *Wild Earth,* was motley matter. *They* were Irish poetry? Then *this* was not. . . . But truly it was. Dramatic, for one thing. For another, recalling Clan Thomas, O Bruadair and Merriman, though these were little known. A diverging Irish poetry, admittedly: human; vehement; unmannered; harsh. It was Stephens.

It was, rather, one part, or at most two parts of Stephens: the teeth in his head, the hard, edged nails of his hands. He would keep them, his nails and his teeth, though more in his stories than poetry; and at last the toothache bawl of Dáibhidh O Bruadair would set James Stephens to scratch him out of his grave. You may find him in a book called *Reincarnations,* complete with bawl and scrawbing talons.—But the scared found solace in other aspects of Stephens: a pigeon's cooing of words; eyes for the moon and the sea. He punched with his fists, and he scratched with his nails; but he stroked with his palms—

and the soft balls of his fingers strummed the strings he
had seemed to tear from the harp with his nails and teeth.
In literal words, they found in him gentle lyricism: the
grace of the world and its light become grace in his line
and syllable. The less endurable passions—jealousy, cruel-
ty, disgust, vengeance—would often rear up horridly; but
intervalled with tenderer spiritual moods. You could see
he was a poet—if perhaps of a rogue-elephant sort. The
intervals were like this:

A long green swell
Slopes soft to the sea,
And a far-off bell
Swing sweet to me,
As the grey, chill day
Slips away from the lea.

That green tree grieves
To the air around,
And the whispering leaves
Have a lonely sound,
As the grey, chill day
Slips away below.

Or like this:

And then I pressed the shell
Close to my ear
And listened well,
And straightway like a bell
Came low and clear
The slow, sad murmur of far distant seas . . .

The intervals were there, but remained intervals. This sort of thing recurred:

> The driver rubbed at his nettly chin
> With a huge, loose forefinger, crooked and black,
> And his wobbly, violet lips sucked in
> And puffed out again and hung down slack:
> One fang shone through his lop-sided smile,
> In his little, pouched eye flickered years of guile.

The very titles—imagine a poem being called *Ould Snarly Gob!* Could The Nine Ladies know such a one?

If the intervals in *Insurrections* left some of the dismayed unsolaced, they surely took heart of grace at *The Hill of Vision* (1912), with its long, ecstatic, Shelleyan *Prelude and Song*: a poem in which that Stephens who, later, fully-ripened, made prose like moonlight of *Etched in Moonlight* and of *Déirdre,* strove prematurely to emerge. *Prelude and Song* was over-fluent; it was watery, to be blunt; but a sign. A sign, I mean, to the consternated, that seas and moons still sang.

While the consternated got confidence, what of the few who had welcomed him molars and all? How did *The Hill of Vision* count with them? They'd been sure he was no mudlark laying slap-bangs on tram-tracks, to pop poor passengers' aesthetic hearts against their poetic palates; quite the contrary, they'd known him for the least-to-be-doubted variety of poet: the man with the load of wisdom; the man with the mind like floodlights; the man who lit up hole and corner, and grass-grown hillside, and sea, soul and salamander, with eyes like headlamps;—and, complementarily, the man whose words were living as worms, wriggling as he picked them up to be bait for readers, the things of all things to make reader-fishes plunge in, curl, and swallow with gust and verve. How did he serve these readers in *Hill of Vision?* Well. They found he had not turned genteel. He had sloughed-off rawness but kept his strength. The teeth were whiter, better-brushed, but still could bite; the nails were trimmed, but still they scratched; the muscles could bunch and spring and the fist still punched. If you're tired of this image of a Stephens red in tooth and claw, here is another one: the whip of *Insurrections* was plaited in *The Hill of Vision;* but it still swished and cracked:

> Now cry, go on, mew like a little cat,
> And rub your eyes, and stamp, and tear your wig;
> I see your ankles! listen, they are fat,
> And so's your head, you're angled like a twig,
> Your back's all baggy and your clothes don't fit,
> And your feet are big.

Every poet with a Joseph's Coat of gifts makes first a book of coloured patches; its colours stand apart and "fight". But if he grows from book to book he learns better tailoring; and Stephens was learning in *The Hill of Vision.* In *Nora Criona,* for instance, whose title is taken from a jig-tune, his dancing rhythm and his Graham Greene sense of the *macabre* click together:

I have looked him round and looked him through,
Know everything that he would do
In such a case, in such a case,
And when a frown comes on his face
I dream of it, and when a smile
I trace its sources in a while.
He cannot do a thing but I
Peep to find the reason why,
For I love him, and I seek,
Every evening in the week,
To peep behind his frowning eye
With little query, little pry,
And make him if a woman can
Happier than any man.

Yesterday he gripped her tight
And cut her throat—and serve her right!

Was ever more economy? Fetch me here a hundred celebrated writers of tales, and let one of them tell *that* tale
with just such thunderbolt blow in five thousand words.
It is one of Stephens's recurrent themes: spouse maddened
by spouse.

Allingham wrote songs for children; Campbell now and
then squatted down in their midst and turned to a child
among them; but, by absolute poetic transmigration, at
hours of his adult existence, Stephens inhabited a "chisel-
er's" skin. His *Seumas Beg* (his own name adapted: that
is the gauge) is no flower-handed pet, but a bundle of ex-
citements, awes, fears, snivels and everything. The bleak,

blasting realism of children is a trait missed always by the lovey-dovey dotards. But Stephens caught it; none better:

> Behind a hill I met a man in green
> Who asked me if my mother had gone out?
> I said she had. He asked me had I seen
> The castle where the people sing and shout
> From dawn to dark, and told me that he had
> A crock of gold inside a hollow tree,
> And I could have it.—I wanted money bad
> To buy a sword with, and I thought that he
> Would keep his solemn word; so off we went.
> He said he had a pound hid in the crock,
> And owned the castle too, and paid no rent
> To any one, and that you had to knock
> Five hundred times. I asked: *Who reckoned up?*
> And he said, "You insulting little pup!"

I could nearly make that poem a text for a total ex-egesis of Stephens's work. His fantasy is there; his child's eyes; his story-telling itch; his way of bashing the spade through the sand-castle; and there is in it a technical thing which many would take to have been first done by younger poets: I mean the writing of verse in words so easy, so natural-footed, that he looks to be scribbling-down what the boy is saying. So far had the doctrine of "the speech of the people" come. The Dubliner especially will wonder how, with hardly a local phrase—except the last, perhaps,—the very go of Dublin talk is given.

The Course of Irish Verse

I have not put myself about to talk of Stephens's fantasy: even our inattentive next-door neighbours expect to get fantasy from the Irish—more than we give them indeed; and Stephens's *Crock of Gold* is—surely it is?—the best-written book of pure fancy in the twentieth century. It is Disney work, if that is not rating Disney too high; and the rumour goes that the *Crock* is on Disney's list of Things to Come. But the extra touch in Irish fantasy—its cold, appalling commonsense like snow on larks' wings—that is what you watch for in Stephens. The philosophers' wives in the *Crock* are made of it; and when it fails in their maker the whole work fails. I judge that his rather repellent poems on God and Satan fail so, fail to be anything really, even blasphemy. They are made-up: Stephens not as the child, but as a book-born *enfant terrible*. They are, not tart, but sourly dull. Yet they show the Irish concern for religion: a constant thing. In Stephens it did not make good poems till his *Kings and the Moon,* his cool, euphonious, stately *Kings and the Moon,* which, ten years after it quietly came out, still waits its due. A. E. would have loved it; it shows his influence; it is dedicated to him; but he died two years before it came. The craft is all Stephens, and, better than any of his verse, this brings together his profundity and that simplicity which never knew *simplesse*. A difficult but a radiant book.

When a poet of multiple gifts has among them the gift for good titles, those titles generally tell us a lot about the man. The titles of Stephens's books of prose would sustain a deal of this character-reading. Consider *The Crock of Gold; Etched in Moonlight; Here are Ladies; The Demi-Gods; In the Land of Youth...* But I contracted to treat here of poetry, not prose, so the titles of his volumes of verse are my only concern. I have alluded already to the title *Seumas Beg,* and remarked its fitness. It is only half the title; the rest being *The Rocky Road to Dublin,* which tells just as much about its author. If I have expanded on *Insurrections* as a title, I now feel fatuous; such titling needs no gloss. But connect *Insurrections* (1909) with *Reincarnations* (1918) and we learn of a change of heart which is worth remarking. If we retitled the book— with much legitimacy—as *Resurrections,* the change would declare itself: Stephens, beginning as a rebel against the immediate past, became a lover of the more remote one. Again the title of a later book, *Strict Joy,* is descriptive of his verse: however much he may seem to *tell* by sheer exuberance and emotional overflow, depend upon it this is the attainment of delicate, inventive and well-poised artistry.

Reincarnations is the one book of those not yet discussed which has decided claims upon discussion in this enquiry. Was it Arthur Griffith (they were quite close friends) who set Stephens learning Irish? It hardly matters; the golden fact is a fact, that he learned enough Irish to take violent, engendering hold on some famous Gaelic poetry; and out of the embraces came two or three translations and a score or more lusty pieces half-Stephens, half-Raftery or O Bruadair or O Rahilly or Keating. The slow emergence of Gaelic poetry into world respect was helped again, by a bag of fine verse that came out of other fine versing. Stephens is not only creative, but Gaelic as well; not only Gaelic but creative as well. I have spent more space than I properly can spare on this space-devouring poet; but another square inch or two must absorb one more quotation. It is from *Clann Cartie,* a poem compounded from more than one of Egan O Rahilly's. Open your throats to say it:

> O Wave of Cliona, cease thy bellowing!
> And let mine ears forget a while to ring
> At thy long, lamentable misery:
> The great are dead indeed, the great are dead;
> And I, in little time, will stoop my head
> And put it under, and will be forgot
> With them, and be with them, and thus be not:
> Ease thee, cease thy long keening, cry no more:
> End is, and here is end, and end is sore,
> And to all lamentation be there end:
> If I might come on thee, O howling friend!
> Knowing that sails were drumming on the sea
> Westward to Eiré, and that help would be
> Trampling for her upon a Spanish deck,
> I'd ram thy lamentation down thy neck.

XXII

ASSUREDLY THE LITTLE I MUST SAY OF FRANCIS LEDwidge would have been not little but much had he not been killed in his twenty-sixth year in Salonika in 1917. Poets stop bullets as efficiently as railway porters or any other sort of men sent abroad for that work, and every war for civilisation sees some of the poets go down. We must keep our fury to ourselves; it is not comprehended by the watch-dogs of universal decency. The intrepid Bernard Shaw, in the midst of a far more jingoistic war than the last one, told Great Britain that to know that a Bill Sykes of England could slaughter a Beethoven of Germany was not a well of undefiled delight to him, Bernard Shaw. But the moral was not drawn when the next world war came on. It was useless—it was indeed somewhat tastelessly funny—for a poet to say, as a reason for not relishing a combative part in the saving of civilisation: *"I am the civilisation for which you are fighting."* Ledwidge was killed in his twenties; it is said he regretted the colours he wore; *we* surely regret that our small resources were lessened by his death.

He did not get time to mature, but had known some success in his work. The success was in part the result of snobbish surprise that a poor manual worker could write good poetry; in part it came to Lord Dunsany's protégé; but in part as well it was earned by a genuine gift, and by its immediate intelligibility in England.

Ledwidge was born in Meath in 1891, and had few chances of schooling, reading, or literary acquaintance, except what Lord Dunsany, a neighbour, gave him at home, and what a while in Dublin put in his reach. The

wonder is, not that he died immature, but that anything
finished remains to fix his name, as a few things do. Poverty, isolation, limited reading and imperfect schooling re-
tard a poet's development, more seriously in a country
with traditions just begun to be restored. We respect him
the more for the measure he achieved. He was certainly
a poet born; but had little more than the landscape of
Meath to make him an Irish poet. Prompt and vigorous
indoctrination, which is normal in a normal community,
and which even in Ireland access to his fellows would
have brought, would quickly have roused in Ledwidge the
sense of the wells, the feeling comprehension of the way
one's nation assists; and, given that, he was another
Campbell or Colum, with a whole new region for his own.
Failing it, his work—for all its promise of quality—has
in it too little which his own five senses supplied.

He did learn quickly, however, and six or seven of his
latest poems show the trend of his mind, a trend displeas-
ing to Baron Dunsany, who excused him for them, on the
ground of the Irishman's generous love of lost causes.
Ledwidge, restive in his khaki, because another colour was
then being worn at home, wrote in verse of much beauty
of the Easter Rising; it is through these poems he properly
joins Irish literature. Not simply that in them his thought
is national; but that, feeling warmly for men with such
history behind them, things were touched in him that nothing had touched before, and his birthright began at last
to serve his verse.

I heard the Poor Old Woman say:
"At break of day the fowler came,
And took my blackbirds from their songs
Who loved me well thro' shame and blame.

No more from lovely distances
Their songs shall bless me mile by mile,
Nor to white Ashbourne call me down
To wear my crown another while."

Overlaid as most of his poetry was by Keats, we never doubt, to use Francis Bacon's word, the "felicity" in Ledwidge. One trait he had, unless I err, which is not the most general in Irish poets: a way of writing of the fields and the rest of the country commonplaces, without violent effect; normally he did not make landscape dramatic, either by stressing its less ordinary features, or by mixing human action into it. In most Irish poetic accounts of scenery or country creatures we are strongly aware of the acts, the thoughts, the sensations and the emotions of men and women, whether these are overtly told or show only in interpretation of scene; but in Ledwidge there is pure, undyed description. Even when he does, in narrative, set men and women in motion on his fields and hills, they do not alter the effect: they are natural creatures, the parts of the scene which have limbs. Perhaps Yeats wrote like this, before Red Dan Philly's bitch was set by Synge to bark men and and women into his pictures. Here is how Ledwidge wrote:

I will brew
Sweet wine of alder for your evening dreams
And pipe you music in the dusky reeds
When the four distances give up their blue.

And when the white procession of the stars
Crosses the night, and on their tattered wings,
Above the forest, cry the loud night-jars,
We'll hunt the stag upon the mountain-side,

Slipping like light between the shadow bars
'Till burst of dawn makes every distance wide.

His verse had always fluidity, euphony and a soft, white light which distinguished it.

XXIII

THOSE "BLACKBIRDS" WHOM LEDWIDGE LAMENTED, THE 1916 poets, what, shall we say, was their purely poetic strength? A hard question for Irishmen (excepting those whom holiness, heroism, or any marvellous thing in the poet will fail to deflect from taking his verse as it is, since to them the absolutes of poetry are settled things). These men's writings have martyrs' blood on their text: their verse, none the less, suggests, to my judgment anyhow, that, Pearse excepted, they were, rather than poets *pur sang,* men of learning and of letters. But then they died in their thirties, possibly before their poetic prime, and we cannot be sure. Of two things about them we *can* be moderately sure: they would, had they lived, have affected our verse and our prose in their philosophic and religious bearings; and they would have made more seminal, more ramifying, direct Gaelic influence upon them.

Why are these things sure?

The first, because Plunkett, MacDonagh and Pearse, all three of them, had Catholic cultivation as well as Catholic sensibility and allegiance. Plunkett and MacDonagh had skimmed the Scholastics, if not read deeply in them; Plunkett, the son of a Papal Count, knew the Spanish mystics; while Pearse, notwithstanding the want in what he wrote of evident acquaintance with Catholic social philosophy, saw all life under sacrament, and owned a spirituality of marked intensity and purity.

The second, because Pearse and MacDonagh knew Irish, vernacular and literary language alike, with something like scholarship.

I considered, up and down in this outline, the relations of Irish poetry and Catholic religion. I seemed to find that in all the nineteenth century only the convert de Vere had high cultivation both in poetry and the Faith. He had that cultivation in poetry, but his hand was too light to make impress on others; and, make it as he might, the advent of masterful Yeats would have smoothed the impress away. Whatever philosophic Catholicism was flowing among Irish writers, Yeats and A. E. and others checked it with counter-thought; they set, in fact, the flow of the stream the other way.

The Course of Irish Verse

Not that Irish Catholics did not make literature. Canon
Sheehan had repute which extended to Europe and
America; he is still respected and read. Katharine Tynan,
whose poetry is undervalued, wrote as a Catholic. The
Catholic vein is in Campbell, and Catholic Colum was
and is. Up to, say, 1910, however, verse in Ireland in the
English language halted at folk-Catholicism. That was
the interest of Plunkett and MacDonagh; they were, as
by no means all writers are, men of intellectual temper;
they knew the cultural compass and the European past
of the Faith; they were not abject in mind, and, therefore,
going to their desks and lifting their pens, they would not
have left their religion in the hall with their gloves. Great
verse or prose they were hardly likely to write; but whatever better makers than they should come from the Catholic Irish, Plunkett and MacDonagh were likely to touch
and tone. After their deaths the fundament of Catholic
culture and conviction was, among artists, rather too light
to hold a house. Joyce, of course, knew such a house in
Europe, but lived outside it, forever peering inside and
writing on the panes. Colum could be rich in knowledge,
yet prefer unknowledgable poetry. While lesser poets were
—lesser poets, and, in matters of intellect, fine-drawn.

It was *queer,* in this weather of opinion, to write poetry
unswervingly and undiminishedly Catholic; as queer as
it once used to be to write Irish poetry. Strange and sharp
to this day is the memory of that mood in Irish writing;
and even now as I say it the poet born Catholic in Ireland
is not by necessary sequence the fellow of Jammes and

Claudel, of Hopkins and Coventry Patmore. I do think, however, that that phase of poetry is over in which exotic or eclectic religions had the best of our verse. Christianity, its creed, its history, the motions and symbols and colours of its rites, and the shapes it gives to men and to men's communities—all these are flowing through our poetry, in Credos and Negos and in indecisive words. It had to come to that, in a nation three-quarters Catholic; but it might have come sooner with Plunkett and MacDonagh and Pearse alive.

Pearse alone of the three wrote in Irish as well as in English. Few in this century but he wrote unqualified poetry in Irish. Some of his pieces—*Fornocht do chonnac thu, Fada liom do theacht* and *Cad chuige dhíbh am' chiapadh?*—suggest a gift for poetry of the order of O Conaire's for the short story. His poems in English are few, but attractive, and of these I should say the best is *A Song for Mary Magdalene*:

> O Woman of the gleaming hair,
> (Wild hair that won men's gaze to thee)
> Weary thou turnest from the common stare,
> For the *shuiler* Christ is calling thee.
>
> O woman of the snowy side,
> Many a lover hath lain by thee,
> Yet left thee sad at the morning tide,
> But thy lover, Christ shall comfort thee ...

Pearse's name has gone some way around the world, and at home it has reverence. His death, and those others, made a difference; so that Yeats who three years before had interred Romantic Ireland—

> Romantic Ireland's dead and gone,
> It's with O Leary in the grave—

found it walking again "amid grey, eighteenth-century houses" and declared

> All changed, changed utterly:
> A terrible beauty is born.

The power to make poetry is rare; when one gets it one is called upon to use it, and normally if the choice be given, no other species of activity should filch one's heart and one's brain and one's sinews away from it. It may even be better, it may be the higher patriotism, in spite of seeming only the more cosy kind, to live and fashion your nation's poetry than to die and leave it poorer in poetry. Was Mangan or Lord Edward Fitzgerald the greater patriot? Which is, the memory of one death or the articulation of one life in viable words, the more splendid endowment? I do not know; and certainly those do not know who find no problem to solve, those to whom the poet's one patriotic function is to metrify opinion, and who, even after he does that, shout him to the tail of the procession, in the rear of the least-effectual "man of action".

Yet even a poet, in a country with no poets to spare, can hardly say the 1916 poets chose wrongly; that they should have lived and made poetry. For, first, they were nobler in moral strength than in strength of art; and, second, the need for their act, its circumstances, and its possibility of fruit were all so great that they more than balance the worth of the verse they'd have made.

It is pardonable, nevertheless, to guess at the poetry Pearse might have made in his forties and fifties. He could write stories; he had tinkered at plays; he had Pericles' double passion, for the ear and for the weal of the people; he had, though an Englishman's son, a love for Irish tradition and Gaelic poetry; he had purity of purpose and compounded well concern for the people with solitary thinking. He had, as an overplus, a dash of the practical worker. Could all these gifts have gone together, and been ruled for poetry . . . But he died instead.

XXIV

HOWEVER LITTLE SYNGE'S TRADUCERS EXPECTED IT, AND however few of them knew or know it, Pearse was of those who defended Synge against odds: "that man in whose sad heart there glows a passionate love of Ireland"; that is what he called him. Pearse saw that Synge had used "strange symbols", but thought that no reason why Synge's fellow-countrymen should pay him back in fiery, coloured words. Pearse was right; but in one way just as right were our fellow-countrymen. At least, if they had to hound Synge, fiery coloured words were the best for him: he himself elected for fiery, coloured words.

And so comes up "John Synge's reverberant name." His original poems are not above a score, yet they must have a word, being strokes of an art very few of whose strokes have not told.

> "It may almost be said that before verse can be human again it must learn to be brutal."

This dictum occurs in the preface to Synge's *Poems and Translations;* and although in a following sentence the author warns us that the poems were written "before the views just stated came into my head", nonetheless it seems plain that, if the views did not generate or form the poems, then the poems prompted or produced the views. In a somewhat forced disclaimer Synge avers that the poems have little to do with the views. I think they have much. Here, from the opening poem in the book, a poem called *Queens,* are lines no other Irishman—except it were Stephens—either could or would have written at the time; which time was 1908-1909.:

> Queens whose fingers once did stir men,
> Queens were eaten of fleas and vermin . . .
>
> •
>
> Yet these are rotten—I ask their pardon—
> And we've the sun on rock and garden.

The Course of Irish Verse

No Gaelic poet would have batted an eyelid at lines like these; many of their company wrote in that very style, and the medieval bite and *danse macabre* were still in their entrails as much they were in Villon's. But Synge's own company, those who poetized around him, were in different case; *they* can hardly have received this *danse macabre*, this God's Acre wit and doss-house waggery, too civilly: "that meditative man John Synge" made strange meditations. Bringing the Gaelic League, the Gaelic Athletic Association and the Dublin Metropolitan Police to the temples of art, the first two strangers to blaspheme, the third to arrest the blasphemers—working this wonder by writing the play of *The Playboy* was right and decent; but *Queens were eaten of fleas and vermin* were not quite vestal virgins for the temples of art. Synge did his singing a bit crudely!

When he turned his hand to the country ballad it was just the same; his sort of ballad was to those of Allingham and Yeats what an all-in wrestler is to a ballerina. *They* had favoured refined lamentations, allegorical lilts of The Silk of the Kine; but Synge's were more like jute bags stuffed with clayey spuds: murderous action-ballads all about men, and not the one half of a dreamy eye among them.

> Then Danny smashed the nose on Byrne,
> He split the lips on three,
> And bit across the right-hand thumb
> On one Red Shawn Magee.

But seven tripped him up behind,
And seven kicked before,
And seven squeezed around his throat
Till Danny kicked no more.

Then some destroyed him with their heels,
Some tramped him in the mud,
Some stole his purse and timber pipe,
And some washed off his blood.

This is Lynchehaun stuff, if not a pre-vision of *No Orchids for Miss Blandish;* a witness's story at the Criminal Court; and that it was a bomb in its day is not to be doubted. Its violence is its weakness; but it must be understood as a thumb to the nose at tapestry-verse. The direction of the nose is clearer in *The Passing of the Shee,* which is not so much crude as rude; its subtitle reads: *After looking at one of A. E.'s pictures.*

Adieu, sweet Angus, Maeve and Fand,
Ye plumed yet skinny Shee,
That poets played with hand in hand
To learn their ecstasy.

We'll stretch in Red Dan Sally's ditch,
And drink in Tubber Fair,
Or poach with Red Dan Philly's bitch
The badger and the hare.

The latter-day friend of both parties laughs twice on reading this—first at the thought of the Celtic Twilight

Poets' hearing their lunar loves described as "skinny"; and second at the equally succulent thought that, having written this, John Synge himself was moonstruck by the lunar loves, and wrote a play about Déirdre.

This poetry of bitch and ditch and rotten queens was part of Synge; a true part; but not all of him. He pitched, when translating, most often on Petrarch and Villon; and the choice tells enough, even forgetting the Notebooks and the nettle-and-nosegay phrases of his plays. Edges and deep lustres he loved, and aimed at making. At first they came separately, but, after a while, together. *Déirdre* has lustre and edge; but he died when he wrote it.

It is one of the best-known facts of our literary movement that Synge was the crest of our wave of popular idiom; "Synge-song" is written and parodied in Ireland and elsewhere. To call his elaborate dialogue synthetic is another way of calling it art; the writer, to borrow a radio image, is the man at the controls, mixing his various "intakes": he is not just a microphone, letting words through as they come. Synge, like Hopkins, and every other writer who finds a forgotten wine-cellar, poured us the wine too eagerly, without decanting; both of them pulled themselves up and cleared the wine, just before dying. To put it plainly, they both were learning plainness.

There was, of course, interaction between Synge and his fellow-artists in Ireland. They acted on him before he did on them; but his was finally the stronger action. Yeats cajoled him out of Paris and packed him off to Aran. Yeats, Gregory and Hyde—but Gregory mostly, it seems —made him smell peasant English; and, after that, Synge's was the blackboard and chalk. Yeats the poet certainly changed through Synge; and the switch in painting, from "Ye plumed and skinny Shee" to Jack B. Yeats's maggie-men, melodeon-players, tinkers, and other picaresque and picturesque earthy species, that is like Synge's doing too— for Synge and Jack Yeats were good friends. Colum and Campbell—and a little later, Stephens—would have had their own bents sharpened—if they were not originally given their bents—by Synge's dominating mind. Higgins, much later again, has much of the rowdy mirth and the frieze-coated language of Synge. A lovely field for *Quod erat demonstrandum*—only that my subject is Irish poetry —would be the native and extra-territorial influence of Synge on prose drama. American and English dialect drama owe plenty to him; and men like Seán O Casey and Eugene O Neill are ink of his ink . . . though the Joycean flood overtook O Casey later.

XXV

THE 1916 RISING MIGHT HAVE SEEMED TO THE BYSTANDER to have been planned as a token revolt, an interim reasser-tion of non-allegiance, and not a full-scale effort at revo-lution. We know that was not true; the full scale was pre-pared though events diminished it; but apart from inten-

tion it was in size and apparent effect a token, no more.
I say apparent effect; because here again the appearance
misled: few events in Irish history compare in moment
with this. We owe the freedom of the greater part of Ireland to the Easter Rising and to what it provoked; and
it follows that our letters was profoundly and quickly affected. Writers had helped to bring the Rising about, and
it was led by poets among others; so influence on poetry
was bound to be a prime effect.

I said *quickly* affected. Yeats responded at once with
the celebrated poem I quoted some pages back: *Easter
1916;* but of course he was not alone. Miss Edna Fitzhenry
has published an anthology of 1916 poems, and most of
the better-known names of the poets of the day are in it.
The quality alike of the Rising and of the poetry of
the time are proved by the artistic interest of the book.
To make a comparison: the *Poems on Spain* compiled in
England after the Spanish Civil War appears to me in-
ferior.

As I stated already, the Rising notably affected Ledwidge; had he not soon afterwards died himself there
would have been loud detonations in his poetry. But Ledwidge was not the only young poet to be sealed; F. R.
Higgins and Austin Clarke, both near twenty in 1916,
took the impress too; and they were beginning to write
just then, so their work from the very outset was Irish
without alloy. These two, Higgins and Clarke, knotted
many strings together; Ledwidge's loss was that few
strings crossed his own in time. The contrast between him-

self and Higgins is licitly made, for Higgins too was a Meathman, though with Mayo blood; and the contrast is that Ledwidge was Irish at the end, but Higgins from the start.

Higgins owed part of the difference to early friendship with Clarke, who, being a Dubliner, lived on the ground where the terrible beauty was born, and, being a student of arts in the National University of Ireland, was taught by one of that beauty's begetters: MacDonagh, lecturer in English literature. Clarke, furthermore, succeeded Mac-Donagh in the post; as student and successor alike he was linked and sealed. We must take MacDonagh's execution as a trebling of the link; for, first to be taught by a man; next to teach where he taught oneself; and third to have his place left open by his death for a cause—this is to link one trebly to him and his truth. Now MacDonagh's cause was liberty for Ireland, and Irish absorption of Gaelic culture; his writing, his lectures and his death taught these; Clarke was among his students; so he taught them to Clarke. But Clarke was intimate with Higgins from early manhood, so Higgins through him encountered the personal force, the embodiment, in combined soldier, poet and scholar, of a set of ideals. Finally, both these fledgling poets, looking about for a master, and being out of sympathy in some degree with Yeats—who was now of an age and a fame to provoke rebellion, and whose rather eclectic doctrine and practice could not content this newly-fired nationality—these young poets pilgrimed to Joseph Campbell in his Wicklow *sheiling;* and there, depend upon it, as Edmund Burke would say, the poet of *Raven's Rock* and of *Irishry,* the friend of Thomas MacDonagh and translator of Pearse's Gaelic stories, did not stint his words on the Rising or the Gaelic world. Torch lights torch; there is never intermission, for intermission is death.

XXVI

WHEN FIRST I MYSELF MET HIGGINS, THEN IN HIS twenty-ninth year, his talk was of O Bruadair and Egan O Rahilly. I knew him better in the closing years of his life; and then as well—after fourteen years—his wish was strong to dip in the Gaelic inkpots. His eyes looked still where he turned them as a boy of twenty.

Higgins's work is a witness at hand, apt and telling as heart could sigh-for, that Irish poets will profit by being last-page Candides, by growing their own potatoes in their own back-gardens; while importing foreign fertilizers when these will help, and importing the grapes and the lemons and the currants and bananas, and all the toothsome fruits our soil won't grow. The making of a national poetry (to go from the top of the earth to its bowels for a change of image) may well be a labour in the mines; but the Jones who goes down with his pick for coal is the Jones who comes up with his paw for pay; while your cosmopolitan writing is more like Nirvana: you pay for its absence of pain by its absence of you. It has always seemed to the Western man to be better to be silly than extinct; just so you had better be a national ass—a frivolous Frenchman, we'll say, or a muzzy German, a blockheaded Englishman or even a priestridden Irishman—than merely to rejoice as a grey, indiscriminate bubble in the thickest, hottest, most mouth-watering cosmopolitan stew. The littler nations cut very little ice while the great big world keeps turning; and the bigger heads in the littler nations shake themselves off their necks at us puffed-up frogs. I recall a master at school who, with weary smile, showed us the smudge on the globe that is known as Ireland; had his teaching been better we'd have pulled his pointer to Greece. . . . Our masters in the school of letters keep their pointers at the smudge; their left hands fondle the continents and seas; and their smiles remain fixedly weary as we babble of green fields. Scouters and doubters will have it that, in this small island, we are much too meagre in minds, in money and in men to hoist a bulk of writing stamped as our own. To this contention Higgins is a hostile witness; if they read him with attention he will give them the lie; of what made his verse, or the differentia of his verse, barely a tithe came from anywhere but Ireland.

That might appear, even to the well-disposed critic, to be carrying nativeness too far; insularity might well be his kindest name for it. Draw, such a critic might say, by all means on your own resources; but will not total dependence on these make underfed work? And yet I think Higgins was right. For the central meaning of this essay of mine, its preponderant thesis, is that after the disintegration of the Gaelic order poetry in Ireland was anything but Irish poetry for many a long day; and that only by multiple efforts and protracted schooling did our poetry approach what should be its normal state: immersion in Irish life; suffusion by Irish life; reaction on Irish life—and finally, a reaching from Irish life to the universal. Countries whose art of letters has always functioned normally will find it immensely hard to conceive our condition, and therefore to understand what we had to do. Broadly speaking we had to do three chief things. First we had to lay hold again on our past. Second we had to make Irish life, in the past and the present, and in all its manifold phases, the matter of our verse. Third we had to acquire a language new to us, and endeavour to make that language take our minds. Now Higgins and Clarke, beginning to make their poetry, began when the effort and schooling were nearly mature: the gates to the past were opening; Irish matter was then an established thing; and Irish ways of writing the English language were more and more being found. It was just then possible to write in an Irish tradition in the English language.

Tradition, if I am an artist, is the suit my father wore. When I'm young I want a brand-new suit for myself, and it seems either hateful poverty or miserly thrift to make me wear my father's suit new-patched. But this particular suit, this native tradition, soon makes up for its patches and old-fashioned cut; the relic of ancient decency is stuffed with wealth. I find gold in the pockets, the lining crammed with bank-notes, and silver pins and diamond brooches caught in the lapels. . . . Irish tradition by Higgins's time was his great-grand-father's, not his father's suit; and the wealth had been hidden away when the family was richer. He tumbled out the wealth like a miser at first, drunk just to see it; but then he started to use it for living and for decorating life; and thus he made it bigger in bulk than it was before.

Higgins had, one might say, two native counties, Meath and Mayo; it is no mere whimsy to add that each matched a side of his heart. The tatterdemalion, sea-bitten, bleak, but multi-coloured and multi-memoried County of Mayo —birthplace of Raftery the poet and landing-ground of the French Invasion of '98—this matched the unsubdued and rakish half of him; while Meath, in its adipose, soft and slumbering richness, suited his second side—his delicateness, his affectionateness, his sloth, his shyness, his dreamy love of ease: having both he had country to give and to take the whole of him. In his first two books—*The Dark Breed* especially—Mayo dominates; he was younger when he wrote them, and youth gets drunk on the fierier stills of the West. But then in his last collection, *The Gap of Brightness*, Meathland at length has jumped the claim of Mayo. In middle-age the Boyne-land of lake-like river, its cattle pampered on the fattest land in the world, its speech as slow as a cloud in a quiet summer, this was the land that he found the most to his taste. The more so as this was uncropped soil for poetry, while the West all poets had ploughed. Yet he *had* the *two* counties. West-

land and Midland were both rich acres and he raised his
verse on both.

Good poets to-day are all but sure to be complex; such
an outline as this must fail to anatomize, fail to tell whole
truths wholly; and here is an instance. To state that Higgins got the West at first hand would certainly be true;
since he lived there when young, and talked, till he died,
of what he saw; yet, quite as truly, he got at the West
through Synge, who had been before him and had brought
his Playboy back. I think I can make this clear.

The West may be seen as a region of soft-voiced people,
a country of subtle colour and half-dumbed sound; and
many who know it well would accept such views. The accent of the County Galway is hard to borrow, lacking that
acute distinction from the general brogue which (the distinction I mean) makes Belfast, Cork and Dublin speech
the actor's prey. This supports the view of unblatant distinction in the West. The West, however, may certainly
be seen quite otherwise—theatrically, violently, gaudily—
and reasonably so. Higgins saw it otherwise, and, seeing it
otherwise, saw it like Synge.

If I make another point the second one supports the
first: Higgins might be nicknamed the Jack B. Yeats of
poetry, for the melodeon-players and the drovers, the tinkers and the motley of the circus, the horses and the jockeys
and the donkeys are all as much at home in his poems as in
Yeats's early pictures: but I said just now that Synge made
Yeats Borrovian. . .

One must not make, however, the younger artist always the debtor of the elder, when they prove to share certain qualities; there is the chance that the younger artist had the thing in himself; *post hoc* is not indubitably *propter hoc*. Thus the romping mirthfulness one finds here and there in Higgins, though Synge has it too, Synge did not give to Higgins; Higgins had it in himself; and if Synge demonstrated its value, as a solvent of the Celtic Twilight, still Higgins did not use it in his way: Synge was sardonically mirthful, Higgins was not, as a rule. The younger man was as gusty in glee as the elder, and *glee* suits the younger man better; Higgins had a stronger vein of pure fun than Synge. As I say it I see him, reminiscently, heave his big belly at a joke, his grey eyes winking and gleaming behind his glasses, and a chain of giggles and chuckles running from his lips like the heave-and-haw-and-gurgle of an old melodeon. Anything less like the melancholy Celt never carried paunch full of poetry—though, of course, he could be mournful or silent like any other man.

I hardly know what does it, but one has a constant sense in reading his poetry that here is a man right down among the people and the fields he wrote of. This means neither of the two things it well might mean, if I did not explain. He was not a doctrinaire middle-class democrat potwalloping with The People on principle, on the one hand; or on the other hand a simple bucolic genius unconscious of his sundering gift: neither of those. With regard to the first, it is true that Higgins had Labour views in politics;

but his politics came from his origins and observation, not from his books; instead of seeking The People on Labour principles, he came to the Labour principles from knowing the people. With regard to the second possible mistake (the ingenuous genius)—however acute his sense of home on a Mayo cross-roads, or walking beside his father on a Boyne-land farm, he was just as certain as Campbell, if need compelled him, to remind strong farmer or go-boy that Higgins was a poet. The headline of Owen Roe O Sullivan would not have escaped him: Owen in a Kerry ploughland at six-pence a day, leaning too long on his spade as he turned his rhymes, but ready for the gaffer who should damn him for an idle rogue. I will talk, thought Owen,

> I will talk to him mildly concerning the Adventure of
> Death,
> And of Grecian battles at Troy left princes downed.

I will tell him, meant Owen, to remember he talks to a poet. Higgins required that that be remembered, too. No, Higgins was a countryman, therefore inside country life, but that was not all. He was a writer as well, leading the double life which gets writing done: that living with half of the self while the second half stares. His being a countryman made him at home in the fields; but the fields were at home in his work through his personal gift. It is this, the personal gift, which defies definition; I cannot so much as show—in small space anyhow—exactly what it did; cannot give enough examples of Higgins's at-homeness. In default I must only *suggest* illustration; while as to explanation, the vaguest phrases must do: that with Higgins, so to speak, our poetry moved nearer to the centre of the Irish ethos.

I begin my suggestion with a general impression. When I think of his second volume, which he called *The Dark Breed*, I immediately experience an atmosphere. Submitting to that atmosphere in memory, I recollect particular words and species of images, with the sorts of gaits his rhythms have, and a general feeling of ancientness. The particular words are *Spain, island* and *Mass, bawneen, poteen, stone-walls;* the rhythms have in them the pacing of clay-caked boots; the images are plentifully drawn, I remember, from waters; and the feeling of ancientness comes in part from the themes, in part besides from sudden flarings of memory. Superadded to these remembrances, I think how physical all seems in him, even when his theme is old eremitical religion. The body's hungers, and its violence in games and labour, are often sung; and the senses of the poet are forever fiercely in action, his sounds and imaginings full of the ear and the eye, and his nerves and his bloodstream seconding the thoughts of his mind. Summoning back these things from the *Dark Breed* poems, a masterful sense of the region they treat of returns to me.

There, perhaps, speaking of this poet's senses and sensuous vocabulary, I have lit on the secret of his power. Higgins is notably sensuous. He can fail in form; he can muddy his total effect; he can hide his sentences' meaning in a nest of boxes; but failing to be sensuous is rarely a fault of his. Rarely does a poem of Higgins's appear to be contrived; he may fail to make, but he does not often make-up. He was, if I do not mistake him, too slothful at once and too lacking in common cleverness, ever to have started a poem which was not self-starting. The poem which he muffs is somewhere about, though not on his page.

The sensuous with him was primarily, though not entirely, a business of images; of visual images first and tactile secondly. More than think things or hear them, he saw them and touched them; pictures and feelings composed the mass of his world. Through the splendour of his gift for phrases we share his senses; we see and touch the world with his eyes and hands. This twofold power, of vigorously sensing, himself, and of sharing his senses through his phrases, is something I can readily exemplify:

> An arch
> That was all of a crouch with the weight of years . . .

> My bent body seemed as an old crane's
> Lost in a great overcoat of wings.

> Were she bred from the silver roots of a well
> Or from the green pulse of a tree
> I'd swear I'd still take her before the high altar
> Of stars to marry me . . .

> Death, the cold skinner of souls . . .

> A lad half-blind in a capful of song.

(This last is peculiarly Irish and very rich in condensed meaning.)

> Our green air grows herbage for healing
> Beneath the cool cheek of the moon.

> Lapp-faced cherubs.

(This to me is a triumph of wording. I recall a copy of Raphael's Madonna which hung over my bed in my childhood; there were two little, fat-faced, bobbed-haired cherubs at the bottom, and *Lapp-faced* they were unquestionably.)

> And here, as in green days you were the perch,
> You're now the prop, of song.

(This is from *To my blackthorn stick.*)

Arguing once full pelt with a friend, a novelist, whether such-and-such a poet was sensuously rich or meagre, and finding one particular thing he asserted difficult to bear, thereupon a horrible suspicion came into my mind. It *was* a horrible suspicion, and I hope a wrong one; but I did suspect the novelist thought *sensuous* meant *soft.* Could he really—if he did, can he still—have no conception that the texture of verse can be brittle and crisp as pastry; as knobbly and dry and rough as the bottom of an elm-bole; as smooth at once and as scored as a skaters' slide; as cold and flowing and glaucous as deep, slow waters? Is it not patent it can? Or is sensuous poetry only the Keatsian fatness; the yielding Spenserean satin; Tennyson's velvet; the sweet, heavy, nectarine ooze of the fruity Nineties? I think it is much more; I *mean* much more when I speak of it in Higgins. Here, for example, is a stanza from *The Blackthorn stick,* from a poem that itself is cut from the flowering sloe:

> Well shod in bronze and lithe with hillside breeding,
> Yet, like a snarl, you dogged my side,
> Mailed in your tridents and flaunting out the fierceness
> That bristled through your hide.

It is nothing if not sensuous, but who will call it soft? You can see the stick; you hurt your hand on it; the spikes prod your fingers, the hard, lithe smooth parts gall your palms. The words have been turned to the timber of the sloe.

This kind of black or white art, whichever it is—and Higgins would have loved to have it doubtful—this kind of Endor or Merlin magicking begins in the arcane soul; but it ends, as may be witnessed, in vowel-and-consonant management. Witnessed it will be.

The fibrous smoothness of the starting line is thus secured it: by placing within it at deciding intervals consonants which half-let the breath drag through them: *Sh* in *shod;* NZ in *bronze;* TH in *lithe* and S in *hillside;* and by assonating *shod* with *bronze,* and *lithe* with *side;* the assonances join the words, giving continuity or smoothness, and contrariwise they emphasize the rough-smooth consonants. The spikiness of the other lines comes from the heaping together of consonants which rasp the breath: *snaRL; doGG'D; mail'D; BRiSTL'D.* While this consonant-placing reproduces the stick's smoothness and spikiness, the bright vowels and frequent verbs reproduce its strength and pliancy.

Here is a second and more varied example of language so adapted to the things of which it speaks that it almost seems as if the things spoke out themselves:

> Cut stone rang with the Lord's name,
> Brass eagles sang His glees,
> The fingered leaves of laurel
> Were folded with His peace;
> Inks ran to hold His knowledge
> While His own scribe adorned
> Stags sheltering in a forest
> Of their own legs and horns.
>
> There lolled those wrinkled craftsmen,
> Whose fingers once unlaced
> The knots of thought in granite
> From God's own hiding-place.

The felicity of those last four lines; the finished style of them! But the whole is admirable; nothing here is just mentioned, but everything fetched-up, taken out of single place and bygone hour and held with all its physicality in viable words; in sounds and in images. Note the Fs, V, Ls, Ss and P in the lines about the laurel, and the words *folded* and *fingered;* the glossy, flexuous feel of laurel is in them.

Note again the GSs and the RNs in the lines about the stags; and the image of the forest.

Not to suggest, by selecting lines of one sort only, that *delicately* sensuous writing is absent in Higgins, I offer another fragment of his verse:

> Wearily veiling
> The air in greys of evening,
> Slow hush of darkness,
> O ease my dreamy pain,
> While violins wheening
> Dreamily on water
> Are waning, waning
> Softly in rain.
>
> •
>
> Hush, woman; no murmur,
> Though moonlight endows,
> Yet stints, windy silver
> On black fruit-boughs;
> No murmur, no sorrow,
> While Time, ebbing by,
> Flickers false moon-dials
> With a swift sky.

That a maker of verse is a true-born poet few signs convince us better than sensuous language, properly and changefully used. Profound and intimate seizure, within the spirit, of bodily being external to itself, produces in the seizing spirit an analogue to body and the dematerialising of objects in the act of knowledge is only a preparation for spiritual rematerialising, or, to avoid paradox

as far as possible, for *resubstantiation* in a deeper knowing act. Mystics speak illuminatingly of *the spiritual senses;*
poets can humbly ratify the phrase: and the sensuous
language of poets is their endeavour to embody, in the
plainer sense of the word, that which has taken substance
in their inward souls. Higgins gives the sign.

Rhythm (as I think) was less surely at Higgins's call
than was figurative language. He told me once his poems
began as images. But to say he lacked rhythmic value
would of course be absurd; it could not be true of a poet
so lyric in mind—"Do poets of your school never sing?"
he asked Louis MacNeice; "Do poets of *your* school never
think?" asked MacNeice again: a profound parable on
Irish and English poetry. It is not true that Higgins lacked
rhythmic value. Skill and variety alike his rhythms have;
and he goes, oftener than not, gracefully, with change-
ful steps, through the changing dances of the Connacht
love-song, the ballad-sheet's tale, the poem of stumbling
dreams, the poem about races, and the modish dance of
half-syllabic verses—as well as walking with sureness in
new speech-metres. Despite this truth, his rhythm is small
in compass when compared with his "high, abounding,
glittering jet" of images. He seldom, so far as I can see,
risked a gallop; and though *Song for a Clatter-bones* syn-
copates as professionally as Haarlem, and *The Ballad of
O Bruadir* has the shanty's sea-legs' roll, still in the main
his verse walks much as he did—musingly and slowly—
even when it carries, as he carried in himself, a big
poem's-load of passion and of brains' adventure.

The Course of Irish Verse

Artistic Ireland, in a long view, "improves with the years"; and a call I made for critics a little while since is looking of late as though it yet might be answered. Heretofore artistic estimation succeeded creation with the ponderous slowness of elephants following birds. I suppose some time we may change our elephants for cats, who will spring and pounce before the birds get away. Till that time comes, a poet so discussable as Higgins must tempt his fellow-poets to discuss and discuss; he tempts me so now; but I must fight back the temptation. I must not, for instance, dilate upon his total Irishness; for one thing my pages are not so many as that needs; for another it would really be very unnecessary work, since every poem he wrote declares him the Irishman—though opinions even vaguely political are hard to find. I must not even investigate his metres fully, revealing how they weave out of older ways of metre, and out of the common, current country speech. The furthest I may go on this line is a word about assonance, in the use in English of which he and Clarke pioneered. Hyde and some others were of course in a way before them; but their use of this central resource of Gaelic prosody, if not quite random, was certainly less systematic, determined and forceful than the use made by Higgins and by Clarke. They were Larminie's first-born, these two, and they held by father; their practice of assonance within and at the ends of lines became almost instinctive.

I give two examples from Higgins; from very different poems.

By the field of the crab-trees my love and I were walking
And talking most sweetly to each other;
In the three-cornered field, we walked in early autumn,
And these were the words of my lover:

•

And softly, softly his words were moving through me—
Coaxing as a fife, crying like a fiddle—
That I heard my heart beat, as dew beats on the stubble;
And the twilight was then lying with us.

There is assonance here not alone in the endings: *walking, autumn; other, lover; fiddle, with us;* but also internally: *field, trees, sweetly* and *field* again; *cornered, walked, autumn; moving, through me; fife, crying, twilight, lying.* It is schematic in the endings, intermittent internally. The second example:

> From black lands we rowed over
> The sacred river Boyne,
> To where saints gaily sported;
> There bagpipes cried with joy
> When all God's walking beauties
> Went by in nun-like robes
> Or played on the grass and coolly
> Slipped naked from their clothes.

Great poets, like great trees, cast massive shadows; poets who grow near them are robbed of their share of the sun; and not till death sets the great bole lying in the grasses does the younger leafage succeed to the beaming of fame. Yeats, and to some extent A. E., obscured the juniors in Ireland—Higgins said it to me once—and Higgins and Clarke were more obscured than the rest. Higgins was Yeats's crony in the latter's old age, and Yeats helped his crony's poems to be known abroad; but Higgins was unlucky in dying soon after Yeats, for his fame would have grown more quickly when the other was dead. It has grown in Ireland; those who read verse read his with a curious love; but abroad he is still less known than his art deserves.

Clarke has been even less lucky; in Ireland he is almost solely a poet's poet (though that's not a title to be despised); while in England the very vanguard neglects his work.

XXVII

Writers often come in twos in Ireland, and Higgins and Clarke ran in double harness for years; how much they had in common their poetry clearly shows—though it quite as clearly shows how far they were sundered.

They shared, to begin with, a Gaelicised theory of verse-craft—one solider in knowledge, one thought-out further, one applied with rarer intermission than their elders' was. For a time they shared, again, predilection for Connacht: first as an isthmus connecting with the Gaelic age; second as décor for poems upon ancient subjects; third as itself a meadow where their verse could browse. It may have been the West—though it might just as soon have been Wicklow—or Meath or Dublin or almost any other place—which made the waters of Ireland enchant these two; but the falling, standing and free-flowing sheets and mountains, thundering or lapping in Ireland by bank or beach, assuredly thunder and lap upon both their songs. Their imaginations (to denote more aspects in common) experienced a recurrent veering to our Middle Age; the habit of the outdoor setting dominates their lines, making them at least in that like the Lays of Finn; their imagery, generally, somewhat excels their rhythm; and both located the pivot of the image in the verb. These are salient likenesses; some fundamental; some reaching out to the detail of style and of craft.

The extent of these poets' alikeness, to those acquainted with both of them, is matter for a measure of surprise; though I speak myself from a late acquaintance with each of them, both being over forty when I knew them well—by which time divergent development would make them unlike.

Unlike they prove, as much as alike, when one comes to dissect their poetry—markedly and pointedly unlike upon many sides.

Take one such side: Higgins was a poet of lyrics; even his dramatic poems are more song than play; whereas Clarke—the epico-dramatist more than the lyrist—in dramatic poems makes play prevail over song.

Higgins, once more, was sensuous, instinctive, emotional; no more intellectual than *every* poet must be; while Clarke, here strongly distinguished, though sensuous and emotional, will not restrict his matter to impression and mood; thought must for Clarke be like things, an object of feeling: he must madder his verse, like Donne, in reason's dye.

Higgins, it is plain, had a gust for adventurous experiment; he was no man's fool at the conscious craftwork of verse; but at stating the aims of experiment Clarke was his better, and his better at articulating a theory's bones.

Contrariwise Higgins had the better of Clarke when they wrote of the country—as both did almost to the total exclusion of the town. The double-sided hedgerow divides their country poetry—Clarke's is the road side, but Higgins's the side of the fields. (Strange that Clarke, a decided Dubliner, has little of the pavement in his work.)

Both Clarke and Higgins could make their verse medieval; but Clarke went oftener back, and sojourned much longer. Perhaps as a corollary, Higgins had the greater "nature", the warmer feeling for people he met in his walks: while for raising the uneasily-interred Clarke's force was much more.

Finally, they differed in ultimate spiritual attitudes. Higgins, a Protestant, found Catholic Ireland poetic, and scarcely wove his own creed into his verse; while Clarke, a Catholic, went like Joyce to the Jesuits, followed him out through their school to his Dublin College, followed him further than that, and to-day is—where?

AT DIFFERENT PERIODS AUSTIN CLARKE HAS WRITTEN three different forms of poetry. He began with narrative poems, epical in style; continued for a time with lyrics, mainly dramatic; and now for some years writes little but "lyric" drama. (Outside verse he wrote two medieval novels, and a number of short slight essays and recollections. These are outside our enquiry.)

Of all the Irish makers of poetry Clarke is among the most conscious and cultivated artists. A relatively slow-minded man, he works elaborately, forging and burnishing verse with endless care. Few have been more than he the literary separatist; though he lived twelve years in England his work is all Irish; on artistic principle—perhaps on prejudice as well—nothing was consciously admixed with his work from England. It is true to say, and illuminating as well, that however intense his ambition for personal eminence—an ambition made almost morbid by unmerited neglect of him—he thinks and works as a builder of Irish culture. Two chief characters meet us in most of his writings, and look like appearing in everything else he may write; they are Clarke himself and a metamorphosed Catholicism. For the Catholic and Roman Church he has taken as his symbol the Black Church in Dublin in whose shadow he was reared.

Clarke, like Yeats, began with mythology. From the Fenian cycle came *The Vengeance of Fionn* and *The*

Sword of the West; from the older Red Branch Cycle *The Cattle-drive of Connaught* and *The Music-healers.* But in treatment he differs decidedly from Yeats, realising in his figures much more of the true epic size, and giving them a much more Gaelic world wherein to move. (He knows enough Irish to make something of the Gaelic texts, though hardly enough to make them his only sources. One or two of his shorter poems are near-translations, and once in a while he made some "oversettings"—to use Mangan's word—or "reincarnations," to use Stephens's—of Gaelic pieces.) What his epics lack chiefly is the art of narration. His personages act significantly only now and then; for the rest they are hollowed and befogged by endless description; till they come by dint of over-writing to loom and gloom like the gods and goddesses in Wagner.

Yet the country of these epics is unmistakably Ireland; and much of the natural description is strong and lovely. Pursuing his discovery that the weather of North-West Europe was first diffused through verse by The Celtic Twilight, he renders the hazy, rainy air of Ireland, its perpetual evanescence of clouds' and mountains' tinting, with arresting, if extravagant effect. As never before, or perhaps since, in poetry, rain drips and splashes and floods and pounds all over his epical page. The false, Italianate sunshine of English poetry is quenched in a brutal flood of Irish fact.

Designing at first to put the whole of the Red Branch Cycle into verse in English, as Stephens earlier designed to tell the whole of it in prose, he left the design uncompleted as Stephens had done, and instead made medieval lyrics for a number of years. These, and especially the book he entitled *Pilgrimage,* constitute a part of the richest work he has done. He wrote in these poems with exceptional distinctness, amounting to idiosyncrasy, which even the casual reader is forced to observe; and in that distinctness is part of the cause of his neglect.

When the black herds of the rain were grazing
In the gap of the pure cold wind
And the watery hazes of the hazel
Brought her into my mind,
I thought of the last honey by the water
That no hive can find.

Brightness was drenching through the branches
When she wandered again,
Turning the silver out of dark grasses
Where the skylark had lain,
And her voice coming softly over the meadow
Was the mist becoming rain.

In this spring-water-music is no echo of anyone, past master or present master; though its welling from the Gaelic rock two things make clear: I mean its permeation with allegory, and its placing of vowels. Higgins, I am sure, discerned how it was made; but only Clarke could have made it: none but he.

It happens that the endings for once are rhymed. They seldom are in the poems of Clarke; for no poet up to his time—not even Higgins—and hardly any since then is so set upon assonance. Here is part of a lyric of his in which a Gaelic *genre*, rather than an actual single poem, is "reincarnated".

AISLING

At morning from the coldness of Mount Brandon
The sail is blowing half-way to the light;
And islands are so small, a man may carry
Their yellow crop in one cart at low tide.
Sadly in thought, I strayed the mountain grass
To hear the breezes following their young
And by the furrow of a stream, I chanced
To find a woman airing in the sun.

Coil of her hair, in cluster and ringlet,
Had brightened round her forehead and those curls—
Closer than she could bind them on a finger—
Were changing gleam and glitter. O she turned
So gracefully aside, I thought her clothes
Were flame and shadow while she slowly walked,
Or that each breast was proud because it rode
The cold air as the wave stayed by the swan.

Strict assonance in endings, and as often as possible within. But he sought to go more fully into the codified metric of *Dán Direach*. I must cite from the note he affixed to his *Collected Poems*:

"In some forms of the early syllabic Gaelic metres only one part of a double syllable word is used in assonance, a system also found in the Spanish ballad metres, and this can be a guide to experiment in partial rhyming or assonance and muting. For example, rhyme or assonance on or off accent, stopped rhyme (e.g. *Win*dow: *thin; horn: morn*ing), harmonic rhyme (e.g. her*o*: Wind*ow*), cross-rhyme, in which the separate syllables are in assonance or rhyme. . .

"In Anglo-Irish folk-verse of the bilingual period assonantal patterns were sometimes used instinctively. Assonance is a complete medium and capable of development, but fails, through excess, if merely used as an addition to ordinary rhyme. Assonance, however, is not an enemy to rhyme. It helps us to respect rhyme, which has been spoiled by mechanical use. By means of assonance we can gradually approach, lead up to rhyme, bring it out clearly, so truly as the mood needs, that it becomes indeed the very *vox caelestis*."

This note, and Clarke's experiments, should interest writers of verse in the English tongue.—*Irish* poets are of course the most concerned; for them they are portion of that salvage from the wreck of Gaeldom which, leading-to and added-to their other autochthonous stores, will make them, properly employed, in truth Irish poets; will preserve them from being no more than John Bull's Other Rhymers.

The note harks back to that phase in our change of language in which the newer tongue had at most supervened on the old, so far as the larger mass of the Irish went. Those in general who took their speech to be English, in truth spoke little of that speech but its single

154

words, and even of those single words little but their meaning: in syntax, idiom and sounds they spoke Irish still. Their folk-songs, as Clarke implies, are in substance non-English; we may say that the popular poetry had a Gaelic soul. Without their intending it, signs of that soul broke-out through the English words; and assonance, to anyone who knows, is just such a sign.—Here we advert to a recent, piquant poetic phenomenon: a second break-through like the first: the sign recurred... The movement to restore the language made the older poetry re-read, and several poets by chance, and here and there, employed assonance in verse. I was one: may I cite my own experience?

Beginning to make verse, I was soaked in Gaelic poetry, and assonance is part of that poetry's age-old dye; so, wholly unaware of Larminie's and Clarke's experiments in vowel-correspondence, and unobservant of Hyde's, which he hardly remarked, I myself mixed assonance with rhyme, both in endings and in innards of lines. I was well at work on my third book of verse before I awakened to this fact. Frank O Connor, I would say from observation of his poems, did exactly as I did, from just the same cause. To-day, besides Clarke, three or four Irish poets use assonance designedly, though of course not with doctrinaire avoidance of rhyme. I myself have had excitement from these experiments, and feel that, *thoroughly explained*—as it has not yet been—assonance would conquer the Englishman's long dislike of it, and greatly extend his range of prosodical resource.

It is time I examined the pioneer use of it by Clarke. Here is a stanza:

> I think it was the food of *Eden*
> We shared, for that *new* ale,
> Though brighter than the serpent-reed,
> Was not indeed of summer's *brew,*
> And drowsily we heard the *calling*
> Of voices from an instru*ment*—
> Soft as the music that *King Saul*
> Had feared beyond his *tent.*

E-den cross-assonates with *pent-reed; new* rhymes with *brew,* in different positions in their lines; *King Saul* crosses with *Call-ing; tent* rhymes with *-ment; reed* cross-rhymes with *-deed;* and *shared* makes internal assonance with *ale.* These are complex correspondences. In *The Young Woman of Beare* they are even more complex, though not all are perhaps schematic.

> Through lane or black archway,
> The praying people hurry,
> When shadows have been walled,
> At market hall and gate,
> By low fires after nightfall;
> The bright sodalities
> Are bannered in the churches;
> But I am only roused
> By horsemen of de Burgo
> That gallop to my house.

To understand the phonetic structure of this stanza examine the touching of the vowels in its accented syllables.

First this structure depends upon the vowel A; upon, to be more specific, a playing on three of the sounds this letter designates. The sound A (as in *cat*) occurs in: *black, shadows,* sod*a*lities, *ban*nered and *ga*llop; and is subtly varied to a slight lengthening of the same sound, in *arch* and *mar*ket. The sound *AI* (as in *pail*) occurs in *lane, arch*way, *pray*ing and gate; and finally the sound AW in *walled, hall* and night*fall.*

Two sounds of the vowel O are played on: the sound OH—shad*ows, low, only* and Bur*go*—and the sound OW: *rouse, house;* and a third sound (as in cot) is placed between OW and OH

> But I am *only roused*
> By *horse*men of de Bur*go.*

There is one rhyme on I: *night* and *bright;* and two on U (as in *hut*): *hurry, Church*es, *Bur*go.

To note that all these occur, and to note their placing, is to find the key to what Clarke is attempting, that is, the pervasion of his verse with multiple sound-correspondences. For further illustration I quote again from this poem:

> I am the bright temptation
> In talk, in wine, in sleep.
> Although the clergy pray
> I triumph in a dream.
> Strange armies tax the south,

Yet little do I care
What fiery bridge or town
Has heard the shout begin—
That Ormond's men are out
And the Geraldine is in.

The lines assonate at the ends in this way: ABABCA
CDCD; and again there is "vowelling" within the lines.

But we cannot continue this peeping at the meshes, and
must be content with the general observation that, up to
his time, none made so massive and resolved an endeavour
to inter-thread with poetry in English the devices of Gaelic
prosody.

Even aside from prosody, we cannot attempt to summarise his work. I will note only salient features in what
remains.

One observes in Clarke the same retarded motion, the
habit of the walker's pace, which we found in Higgins;
and he walks more slowly still than the pondering Meathman. In earlier poems—*The Cattle-drive in Connacht* for
example—there are quick-footed lines; but these, insofar
as I studied them, all have quick, bodily movements for
their theme, and so are on the primary level of onomato-
poeia. Of the words which recur in Clarke, *thought* is
possibly most frequent; most of his "matter" is treated at
the level of thought (though thought *experienced* of
course); and this induces a musing tone in his verse. That
word *experienced* is vital; everything, even thought, with

Clarke is sensuous; and the sensuous words with their load of smouldering intellect make strongly individual work. But, again adverting to motion, there is little of the hurtle of ideas in this poet's verse; one thought or two, rather, held under focussed lenses, and kept tenaciously there till the smouldering begins. He is hardly a Robert Browning or even a George Meredith. He is scarcely a philosopher at all, in his verse or outside it.

He has on the other hand a signal feeling for particular epochs of our history—though he views those epochs in a way not many have done. (That forbidding Black Church, alluded-to earlier, extends its shadow over many of his pages; and even the scripted vellums of our Golden Age, so delicately lettered, and lacquered with such gorgeousness, in inks of violet and scarlet and ochre and gold, not even these must be symbols of illuminated minds. The Catholic Church, in Austin Clarke's imagining, has beauties like altar-vessels and tabernacle lamps; but the church itself is darkened, and these are only tingeings on the gloom. Liturgical hues may change to suit the season; but his mind will muffle the purple and white with black.) To return: the poem I have just now quoted—*The Young Woman of Beare*—exemplifies his feeling for the amplitude of myth, as it merges in his feeling for the chronicled advance of history—with the topical overtones added to make all present-day. He employs the successive lives of the Woman of Beare as conduits to carry one stream of our spiritual history: what he himself has named our "drama of conscience". It is one of his finest achievements, and one of the most striking and grandly-conceived of our poems.

François Mauriac, a master of the "drama of conscience", avers that the writer hands himself over in his books. Few can have more opposed that delivery than Clarke. Few of his poems are immediately personal; rather than speak as *I—I, Austin Clarke*—he has sought what Eliot named "the objective correlative": such fable, character, or incident of history as, carrying his experience, would depersonalise it; or maybe enable him to go *incognito* inside it. More than any of his books his small *Night and Morning* is he himself as a person saying his say. But in it he speaks so arcanely, lurks and skulks in such pitchy corners of language, that what he says is often matter for debate.

> No story handed down in Connaught
> Can cheat a man, nor any learning
> Keep the fire in, turn his folly
> From thinking of that book in Heaven.
> Could I unbutton mad thought, quick-save
> My skin, if I were caught at last
> Without my soul and dragged to torment,
> Ear-drumming in that dreadful place
> Where the sun hides in the waters?

This is not one of his most teasing stanzas; still, though one can, with a certain confidence, conjecture its general drift, and some of its detail, details remain which obstruct entire understanding. What is the *full* force of "Keep the fire in"? "Unbutton"? "Ear-drumming"? (For, Clarke's phrases always *intend* to be richly relevant, and erudite punning is one of his devices.) We may surmise, but hardly be sure. So, when whole poems consist of such obstructions our understanding is firmly baulked. Readers are of varied hardihood; but for most this layering and obscuring of meaning requires excessively strenuous digging. Pick and shovel are tools of hard labour, and the bent for excavation is rare.

I would never deny, notwithstanding, that gain there is from this intent, impelled contemplation which made *Night and Morning*. The last flicker of that spiritual levity which pestered Anglo-Irish verse, which in Millikin and Lever made a circus of a persecuted people, which evinced itself in Yeats as dalliance with the picturesque in faith, which in Higgins became *Carpe Diem,* the gallivanter's roystering, that last flicker dies out under Clarke's *Dies Irae.* Sombreness like his, in Ireland, no poet has had for generations; Clarke is as serious-souled as Egan O Rahilly.

1930 to 1938 was Clarke's least fertile period in verse; the twelve poems of *Night and Morning* are all the new verse he published in those eight years. In 1939 he began broadcasting regularly from Radio Eireann; in 1940 he and I founded The Dublin Verse-Speaking Society, which later became The Lyric Theatre Company—now controlled by him alone—and in these two beginnings Clarke found renewed stimulation. Between 1939 and 1946 he wrote, produced and published seven short plays in verse, one for broadcasting and six for the theatre.

He, more than any Irish poet for some decades, agreed with Yeats, that the poet must once more stand among the shafting lights of the stage, for his own and the theatre's salvation. He had written two plays before the seven I mentioned, a one-act, and a short three-act. The themes of his plays are variously derived: from Gaelic mythology, medieval satire, folklore, and French comedy freely adapted. In them is visible also, though with a difference, that movement from lavish lacquering of surface to agonised pondering on the soul which we observe in his poems. The difference is the presence of humour in the plays. Though the core of each is gravity, only three— *The Plot is Ready, Sister Eucharia* and *The Flame*—are free of the guise of comedy or farce.

Clarke first began to laugh when he turned to the play. *The Cattle-drive in Connaught* has some spurts of humour, but his jaws creased deeply first in *The Son of Learning*. The ancient texts on which he based them had humour, and he was so free of the Celtic Twilight as to relish and sustain their laughter. It may seem, then, perverse exposition to speak of agonised pondering in relation to his plays. But the humour of Clarke, however amusing, is seldom light-hearted through and through. He is even more sallowly sardonic than Synge, and his laugh trenches lines from the nostrils to the corners of the mouth. When Clarke the poet laughs, somebody smarts; or if not, then the poet has an extra chuckle at his cunning.—Even the most airy and bubbly of his plays—*The Kiss, The Second Kiss, The Viscount of Blarney*—, with their light, bright words, their feathery metres, their toying with pierrot and pantomime machinery, even these bob within a cumulus of shadow, and the apples of the knowledge of good and evil sway among the sun-dazzled leaves. Put all else aside but the profit of the plays, and the dark underside of his words is mismanaged craft: for, willy-nilly, the audience lets it by or gropes for it blindly. Yet, shadows or no, underside or no, humour he has, and credit he must get for it. He acted against the widely-accepted tenet, that poetic plays must strut and attitudinise, talking all the time of "the cloudy symbols of a high romance". He was not, indeed, the first of his century's Irishmen to parcel poetry and laughter together for the stage; Synge and Fitzmaurice had done it in imaginative prose, and Yeats now and then in prose and in verse—*The Player Queen* and *The Green Helmet*. But in Ireland and elsewhere in modern times the pressure of custom was hostile to humorous poetic drama, until Clarke began laughing in prosody.

His passion for the battens and the cycloram is changing his verse, as it did that of Yeats and of any other poet it seized on; for example, it has led him back to the couplet, and to rhyme. However, he professedly disavowed the abjuration of rhyme, in that note to his *Collected Poems* which I quoted above; so we must not infer from his recent practice that he has now abjured assonance. I confess to curiosity as to the kind of lyric or narrative verse Clarke would now write, for I fancy he will write other things than plays in the future, even though plays still come from him. It is noteworthy that one of the best lyrics he ever made occurred in the one play he wrote for broadcasting: *As the Crow Flies*. Here it is:

> Stop, stop and listen for the bough top
> Is whistling and the sun is brighter
> Than God's own shadow in the cup now!
> Forget the hour-bell. Mournful matins
> Will sound, Patric, as well at nightfall.
>
> Faintly through mists of broken water
> Fionn heard my melody in Norway.
> He found the forest track, he brought back
> This beak to gild the branch and tell, there,
> Why men must welcome in the daylight.
>
> He loved the breeze that warns the black grouse,
> The shouts of gillies in the morning
> When packs are counted and the swans cloud
> Loch Erne, but more than all those voices
> My throat rejoicing from the hawthorn.
>
> In little cells behind a cashel,
> Patric, no handbell gives a glad sound.
> But knowledge is found among the branches.
> Listen! The song that shakes my feathers
> Will thong the leather of your sandals
>
> Stop, stop and listen for the bough top
> Is whistling . . .

It is a free translation of a Fenian lyric, *Binn sin a Luin Doire an Chairn,* but done as only Clarke could do it. It is one of those heart-raising rewards a poet sometimes gets for years of stony experiment, which seem to the bystander wilful and harmful forcing of theories. This lyric could be the subject of a long, luminous analysis, but I will say no more here than this: that every vowel, and every rest fit into place here like pieces of stained-glass, and that the thought and feeling come through like sunlight to make all the colours glow. It is as Irish as Cormac's Chapel in Cashel, something the world has had from us, and would not otherwise have found.

It is to be remarked that Clarke is barely fifty. Given the "allotted span" and continued productiveness he cannot fail to be one of the most unusual poets in our history.

XXIX

HE IS THE LAST POET I SHALL EXAMINE HERE. THIS BOOK is an outline, not a history, of Irish poetry in English; I have omitted mention of a number of poets of the past and present lest I should overcrowd; and for this and other reasons I intend to do no more than allude to Irish poets still under fifty.

In England the best-known of Irish-born poets under fifty are probably Louis MacNeice and Cecil Day Lewis. Day Lewis is, despite his birth, perhaps more English than Irish in all his family origins, though he is, I believe, re-lated to Oliver Goldsmith; so we must allow him to be naturally an English poet. MacNeice, born in Belfast, of Irish family, is almost wholly Irish in origin; but almost wholly English in his work. In him the tradition of voluntary transplantation has its latest notable example. He has written poems with Irish subjects and some Irish feeling; but all told he is an English poet so far.

Among the poets who are physically and spiritually residents of Ireland we may name: Patrick Kavanagh, Monk Gibbon, Patrick MacDonogh, Pádraic Fallon, Donagh MacDonagh (son of Thomas), W. R. Rodgers, John Hewitt, Roy MacFadden, John Lyle Donaghy, Blánaid Salkeld, Richard Rowley; and perhaps I may be permitted to add my own name.

It might be assumed by any reader of this book who is unfamiliar with contemporary Irish poetry that their work is not only totally Irish in matter, technique and tone, but predominantly Gaelic in its influences. I do not think the truth is quite that. Literary communications, like others, have become closer and quicker in the modern world; besides, there have been violent innovations in modern poetry; and Irish poetry, no less than that of other countries, reflects these changes. The influences of Eliot, Pound, and their English juniors has penetrated to Ireland; Hopkins's strong hand has been laid on us as on others; and Chesterton has not quite passed us by.

"Influence" is a word used vaguely in criticism. It is to be hoped that Irish poets will never cease to read the poetry of other countries and to absorb and adapt to their own ends whatever other countries have to teach them; but this must be done as the body absorbs and transforms its food—as a means of nourishing a poetry which remains our own—: it is scarcely a sign of rude health if a tiger's body turn into a lion's. *That* would not be in the order of natural events, and the tiger's body could not be said to be finding its greater perfection.

Irish poetry on the whole, and certainly in its better part, is decidedly Irish. This book has made clear what I suggest by the epithet; but I may mention a very healthy sign of our condition which is not so very old as to be unremarkable. It is this: Irish poets and writers are now in the habit of assessing their work against the background of other Irish writing, instead, as was formerly the case, of measuring it against the work of English poets and writers. It is the comparison and contrast of X. Y.'s poems, plays or stories with the poems of Yeats or Stephens, the plays of Synge or Lady Gregory, the stories of Seumas O Kelly or Joyce—it is these comparisons and contrasts which are now made at first; and I, who am not an ancient, can remember when it was not so.

There have been among younger poets the customary rebellions. Some were so much in revolt against their elders, and so fetched by the louder music of English and American literary concert-halls, that they walked right out of their own doors, trying to be at home across the street. They seemed to want to write like the Eliots and the Audens. It would not be true to claim that they all came back to their own house; but the signs are strong that they are one by one returning; and if one or two are loitering still on the pathway, the family voices are not failing to reach their ears.

In this connexion the poets of the North-East are especially interesting. Partition has by now become spiritual in some of those who live in the Six Counties; and a poet like John Hewitt is strongly aware of his position. But all that we mean by Ireland is holding them from absorption into English poetry; and if the grip can be seen in Hewitt it has all but succeeded entirely with Rodgers. A markedly Irish temperament and a love of the Irish country keep him with the covey. His recent removal to London may have its effect, but we shall see.

In the Twenty-six counties of course the Irish ethos works more vigorously. Self-Government and all that produced and flows from it, help our literary separatism, which we believe in not because it is separatism but because it is the habit of all healthy nations. Did Goethe, Villon, Dante, Ibsen, Johnson, Calderon lose or gain as writers through being wholly German, French, Italian, English, Norwegian, or Spanish, each his own?

Patrick Kavanagh is possibly the first poet of several generations who literally broke Irish soil for seed; Donagh MacDonagh had for father one of those who died against a wall for "the intellect and the immortal soul of Ireland," which he had already sung, and studied in critical prose; Pádraic Fallon is of Catholic stock from the country of Raftery and the Love-Songs of Connacht; and so we might show of each that in his purse he carries coin for purchasing. We share Ireland and the Irish poetic tradition among us; and most are unlikely to forget that it is good. It is my hope that this short book will make clear, in some degree, in what that tradition consists, and what labours of restoration and innovation have given it to us. May our labours, under God, continue it, strengthen it, and pass it on to the poets who come after us.

BOOKS FOR FURTHER READING

A. *Criticism and history:*

Aodh de Blácam: A First Book of Irish Literature.
Ernest A. Boyd: Ireland's Literary Renaissance.
Hugh A. Law: Anglo-Irish Literature
Stephen Gwynn: Irish Literature and Drama.
W. B. Yeats: Essays. Autobiographies.
George Moore: Hail and Farewell.
Alfred Perceval Graves: Irish Literary and Musical Essays.
Thomas MacDonagh: Literature in Ireland.

B. *Anthologies:*

Brooke & Rolleston: A Treasury of Irish poetry.
John Cooke: The Dublin Book of Irish Verse.
Lennox Robinson: The Golden Treasury of Irish Verse.
Alfred Perceval Graves: The Book of Irish Poetry.
Donagh MacDonagh: Poems from Ireland.
Eleanor Hull: The Poem-book of the Gael.
Geoffrey Taylor: Irish Poems of To-day.
Kathleen Hoagland: A 1,000 Years of Irish Poetry.
Edna Fitzherbert: A 1916 Anthology.

C. *Individual poets:*

James Clarence Mangan: The Poems of James Clarence Mangan.

Allingham: Songs, Ballads and Stories.

Larminie: Fand and Other Poems.

Hyde: Love-Songs of Connacht.

Yeats: Collected Poems. Collected Plays.

A. E.: Collected Poems.

"Seumas O Sullivan": Collected Poems.

Joseph Campbell: The Mountainy Singer. Irishry. Earth of Cualann.

Pádraic Colum: Collected Poems.

James Stephens: Collected Poems.

Francis Ledwidge: Collected Poems.

Synge: Poems and Translations.

F. R. Higgins: Island Blood. The Dark Breed. The Gap of Brightness.

Austin Clarke: Collected Poems. Night and Morning. Black Fast. Sister Eucharia. As the Crow Flies. Three Plays.

Monk Gibbon: For Daws to Peck at. Seventeen Sonnets.

Patrick Kavanagh; The Ploughman and Other Poems. A Soul for Sale.

Donagh MacDonagh: Veterans and Other Poems. Happy as Larry.

Patrick MacDonogh: Over the Water. The Vestal Flame.

John Lyle Donaghy: Into the Light. Selected Poems.

John Hewitt: Conacre.

W. R. Rodgers: Awake and Other Poems.

Richard Rowley: Ballads of Mourne.

Blánaid Salkeld: Hello Eternity. . . the engine left running . .

The Course of Irish Verse

Roy MacFadden: Swords and Ploughshares. Flowers for a
Lady.

Robert Farren: Thronging Feet. Time's Wall Asunder. This
Man Was Ireland. Rime, Gentlemen, Please.